# GETTING
# DENSITY
# RIGHT

## Tools for Creating Vibrant Compact Development

**Urban Land Institute**

**NMHC** National Multi Housing Council°

ULI–the Urban Land Institute
1025 Thomas Jefferson Street, N.W.
Suite 500 West
Washington, D.C. 20007-5201


**Library of Congress Cataloging-in-Publication Data**

Getting density right : tools for creating vibrant compact development.
     p. cm.
 Includes bibliographical references.
 ISBN 978-0-87420-083-6
 1.  City planning—United States—Case studies. 2.  Community
development, Urban—United States—Case studies.  I. Urban Land
Institute.
 HT167.G47 2008
  307.1'2160973—dc22

2008000404


10 9 8 7 6 5 4 3 2 1
Printed in the United States of America.

**FSC**
**Mixed Sources**
Product group from well-managed
forests and other controlled sources
Cert no. SGS-COC-004394
www.fsc.org
© 1996 Forest Stewardship Council

## About ULI–the Urban Land Institute

The mission of the Urban Land Institute is to provide leadership in the responsible use of land and in creating and sustaining thriving communities worldwide. ULI is committed to

■ Bringing together leaders from across the fields of real estate and land use policy to exchange best practices and serve community needs;

■ Fostering collaboration within and beyond ULI's membership through mentoring, dialogue, and problem solving;

■ Exploring issues of urbanization, conservation, regeneration, land use, capital formation, and sustainable development;

■ Advancing land use policies and design practices that respect the uniqueness of both built and natural environments;

■ Sharing knowledge through education, applied research, publishing, and electronic media; and

■ Sustaining a diverse global network of local practice and advisory efforts that address current and future challenges.

Established in 1936, the Institute today has more than 40,000 members worldwide, representing the entire spectrum of the land use and development disciplines. ULI relies heavily on the experience of its members. It is through member involvement and information resources that ULI has been able to set standards of excellence in development practice. The Institute has long been recognized as one of the world's most respected and widely quoted sources of objective information on urban planning, growth, and development.

## About NMHC–the National Multi Housing Council

Based in Washington, D.C., National Multi Housing Council represents the largest and most prominent firms in the apartment industry, including owners, developers, managers, lenders and brokers. The Council benefits from a focused agenda and a membership that includes the principal officers of the most distinguished real estate organizations in the United States.

For more than 25 years, NMHC has provided strategic leadership to the apartment industry through its highly effective government affairs program, its business guidance and research reports, and its public affairs program.

NMHC serves as the apartment industry's primary advocate on legislative and regulatory matters. The Council concentrates on public policies that are of strategic importance to participants in multifamily housing, including housing and finance, tax, technology, property management, environmental issues, regulatory barriers to apartment construction and building codes.

In addition to providing leadership on public policy issues, NMHC is acknowledged as the preeminent source of apartment-related information. The Council is committed to expanding the scope of industry research by conducting and sponsoring research that assists apartment firms make critical business decisions, improves the industry's policy and regulatory environment, and provides consumers with full information on their housing choices.

## Review Committee

**Conrad Egan**
*President and Chief Executive Officer*
National Housing Conference
Washington, D.C.

**Con Howe**
*Managing Director,* Los Angeles Fund
CityView
Santa Monica, California

**John K. McIlwain**
*Senior Resident Fellow*
ULI/J. Ronald Terwilliger Chair for Housing
Urban Land Institute
Washington, D.C.

**Nicolas P. Retsinas**
*Director*
Joint Center for Housing
Harvard University
Cambridge, Massachusetts

**Kate White**
*Executive Director*
ULI San Francisco
San Francisco, California

## ULI Project Staff

**Rachelle L. Levitt**
*Executive Vice President, Global Information Group*

**Dean Schwanke**
*Senior Vice President, Publications and Awards*

**Richard M. Haughey**
*Director, Multifamily Development*
*Project Director*

**Jason Scully**
*Senior Associate,* Development Case Studies
*Project Director*

**Theodore Thoerig**
*Associate*
*Project Associate*

**Nancy H. Stewart**
*Director, Book Program*
*Managing Editor*

**Lori Hatcher**
*Director, Publications Marketing*

**Laura Glassman,** Publications Professionals LLC
*Manuscript Editor*

**Betsy VanBuskirk**
*Art Director/Book Designer*

**Anne Morgan**
*Graphic Design*

**Craig Chapman**
*Director, Publishing Operations*

**Karrie Underwood**
*Administrative Manager*

**Devon Horne**
*Intern*

## Authors

### Introduction
Richard M. Haughey

### Tools at a Glance
Theodore Thoerig
Richard M. Haughey
Deborah Myerson
Jason Scully

### Community Case Studies
**Mike Baker**
*Los Angeles, California*

**Clair Enlow**
*Seattle, Washington*

**Jennifer LeFurgy**
*Alexandria, Virginia*

**Deborah Myerson**
*Bloomington, Indiana*

**Sam Newberg/Joe Urban, Inc.**
*Minneapolis, Minnesota*

### Tools for Success
Deborah Myerson

## Acknowledgments

This publication results from an ongoing partnership with the National Multi Housing Council in support of our joint interest in fostering compact development as an integral component of smart growth. ULI would like to thank and acknowledge Doug Bibby and his team, including Kim Duty and Michael Tucker, for all of their input and guidance. Special thanks are also due to the review committee: Conrad Egan, Con Howe, John McIlwain, Nic Retsinas, and Kate White, whose real-world experiences helped keep this book from being too theoretical.

Deborah Myerson played an important role in shaping this publication, both conducting the research for the toolkit and authoring a case study. Mike Baker, Clair Enlow, Jennifer LeFurgy, and Sam Newberg did an excellent job covering the remaining case studies. Thanks to Jason Scully and Ted Thoerig for picking up the manuscript and running it across the finish line after my move to ULI's Western Region Office in Los Angeles. And thanks also go to Rachelle Levitt, Dean Schwanke, Lori Hatcher, Nancy Stewart, Betsy Van Buskirk, Anne Morgan, and all of the additional ULI staff responsible for making this publication a reality. Finally, thanks to Devon Horne, ULI intern, who assisted with research during her summer internship. So many people pitched in to help that I apologize to anyone that I missed. I hope this publication helps move the discussion of compact development from the question of "why?" to the answer of how.

Richard M. Haughey
*Director, Multifamily Development*

# Contents

**1. INTRODUCTION** ..................................................**3**

Profiled Communities ...............................................6

Keys to Success .......................................................8

**2. TOOLS AT A GLANCE** .............................................**17**

**3. COMMUNITY CASE STUDIES** .....................................**31**

Huntersville Zoning Ordinance,
    Huntersville, North Carolina ...............................32

Downtown Redvelopment, Evanston, Illinois...........39

Plantation Midtown District,
    Plantation, Florida ............................................47

New Model Colony, Ontario, California ...................57

Columbia Pike Form-Based Code,
    Arlington County, Virginia ..................................67

Downtown Zoning Changes,
    Seattle, Washington ..........................................74

University Neighborhood Overlay,
    Austin, Texas ....................................................88

City of Villages, San Diego, California ....................94

**4. TOOLS FOR SUCCESS: ACHIEVING COMPACT
DEVELOPMENT AND HIGHER DENSITIES** ...................**103**

Codes .............................................................. 104

  Form-Based Codes ......................................... 104

  Model Codes .................................................. 106

  Renovation Building Codes .............................. 108

Zoning ............................................................. 111

  Mixed-Use Zoning ........................................... 111

  Planned Unit Development ............................... 112

  Overlay Zones ................................................. 113

Development Types ............................................ 115

  Brownfields Redevelopment ............................. 115

  Cluster Development and Conservation
    Subdivision Design ....................................... 117

  Infill Development ........................................... 119

  Traditional Neighborhood Development ............. 120

  Transit-Oriented Development ........................... 121

Density and Design Tools .................................... 125

  Accessory Housing and Cottage Housing ........... 125

  Design Review and Design Guidelines ............... 126

  Development Rating Systems ........................... 128

  Financial Incentives ........................................ 131

  Transportation Demand Management ............... 134

  Street Classification and Design ....................... 136

Planning and Visioning ....................................... 138

  Community Visioning Workshops
    and Charrettes ............................................ 138

  Density Visualization ....................................... 140

  Transect-Based Planning ................................. 141

**BIBLIOGRAPHY AND RESOURCES** ............................**142**

# GETTING
# DENSITY
# RIGHT

## Tools for Creating Vibrant Compact Development

# Chapter 1

# Introduction

DEMOGRAPHIC SHIFTS, HIGH INFRASTRUCTURE
and construction costs, population growth, the long-term out-
look for energy, and anticipated climate change make more-
compact development inevitable, despite lingering public
opposition to higher density. In many growing, urbanized
communities, the debate over whether to build compactly—up
rather than out—is over. For these communities, the debate is
now over where to increase density and how best to encourage,
facilitate, plan, and design new compact development.

This book is written for land use professionals in rapidly growing communities. It is more technical how-to guide than tome on the virtues of compact development. The intended audience includes community leaders, planners, developers, architects, and elected officials who wish to create and enact regulations that will encourage compact development in their communities. Their reasons for doing so are plentiful: reducing traffic congestion and harmful carbon emissions, preserving open space, using public infrastructure better, more efficiently using public investments and services (including mass transit), integrating pedestrian and bicycle access to new developments, increasing property tax revenues, or just simply creating great places.

The three major sections of this book are an introduction and overview, eight case studies of communities that have changed their regulations to facilitate compact development, and a collection of policies and programs from around the country that are being used to encourage and facilitate compact development. We call this last section the toolkit.

Immediately following this introduction we have included a table that lists all of the case studies and policies mentioned in the subsequent chapters. This table includes pertinent information on the program type, location, implementation date, as well as a brief description of each resource.

Premised on the belief that a consensus has emerged among land use professionals and a growing segment of the market in support of appropriately located compact development as an antidote to sprawl, this book supports the growing realization that compact development is a desirable way to respond to volatile energy supplies and climate change. Numerous studies demonstrate that compact development can reduce the number of vehicle miles traveled (VMT).[1] Reducing VMT corresponds to lower greenhouse gas (GHG) emissions. Lowering GHG emissions is imperative to halt the potentially

catastrophic effects of climate change. Moreover, an important, and possibly surprising, fact is that daily commutes produce only 20 percent of the total VMT in a region.[2] So although compact mixed-use infill near places of employment holds the most promise for reducing VMT, significant reductions in VMT can be accomplished through compact development even when people are not located within walking distance of their jobs. Reducing the distance between homes and grocery stores, schools, dry cleaners, movie theaters, and restaurants will correspondingly reduce VMT along with GHG emissions. Ideally, having these uses within walking distance can reduce the VMT to zero (and create a healthier and higher quality of life), but just reducing average VMT reduces GHG emissions. Simply put, compact mixed-use development allows us to spend less time in our cars running errands and could help save the planet—not a bad combination.

Although the arguments for compact mixed-use development are convincing, the reality is that many people oppose almost all new development, and that opposition often increases with the density of the proposal (and its proximity to their property). To address this issue and the many misconceptions that exist about compact development, we have dedicated a portion of the toolkit to building community support for compact development through community visioning, planning, and participation.

Without an educated public that fully understands the effect of population growth and the consequences, challenges, and trade-offs inherent in land use decisions, support for regulations encouraging compact development will suffer. The benefits of compact development and the negative consequences of low-density development may not be readily apparent to the public, which often mistakenly blames density for the consequences of a low-density development pattern. Without a complete understanding of how land use affects the environment, a community may not attain the goals it is seeking. For example, a community that sets a goal of open-space preservation may prohibit compact development, assuming that higher densities are a threat to its open space. The more likely reality is that low-density development (using a large amount of land to provide relatively few housing or commercial uses) is the greater threat to its open space. Compact development constrains development to a smaller area, allowing preservation of the outlying areas as open space. Such misunderstandings of the benefits and consequences of land use decisions are unfortunately all too common.

Addressing the many misconceptions about compact development is an important part of developing the community consensus required to create and enact policies and programs that support compact development. Overcoming these misconceptions is the first step toward creating solutions and enacting regulations that realistically address anticipated population and job growth and a dwindling supply of developable urban land.

Of course, another important part of the process is accepting the inevitability of that growth. Young couples continue to have children, and people from all corners of the world continue to flock to America for the economic opportunities the country provides, creating significant population growth. The U.S. Census Bureau projects that America will add almost 55 million new residents between 2010 and 2030, roughly 2.7 million new residents per year. Because this growth has been and will likely continue to be distributed unevenly throughout the country, the accepting communities will be significantly affected. High-growth communities that fail to accept this reality too often also fail to plan for it. Their failure to plan, in the end, gives them more of the same type of development that they consistently complain about: low-density sprawl that clogs their schools and roadways, pollutes their air and water, and gobbles up their agricultural lands and open space.

Denial is not an effective growth management strategy. Another alternative exists. Developing more compactly provides communities the opportunity to maximize the return on their public investment in infrastructure, preserve their agriculture and open space, create walkable communities,

COURTESY OF VAUGHN WASCOVICH

**Compact site design allows more land to be preserved for open space and recreational amenities.**

connect their road network with their public transportation and bicycle networks, and create vibrant places. With single-person households and empty nesters representing the fastest-growing household types, demand exists for such vibrant places. The convenience, amenities, and services provided by compact development can promote a lifestyle that is attractive to this demographic.

This book can help. The eight case studies provide excellent examples of communities that have chosen to develop more compactly. These profiles tell how they built community support for compact development and how they changed their land use regulations to make it happen. The toolkit portion of the book provides policy and program tools that can be used individually or together to encourage and facilitate compact development. With more compact development inevitable, we hope this book will continue the discussion on how we can grow smarter and avoid some of the land use mistakes we have made in the past.

# Profiled Communities

The eight communities profiled in this book have decided that more-compact development makes sense for a variety of reasons, and they have successfully enacted new regulations to support it. The communities range in size from small to large and represent just about every region of the country. From Seattle, Washington, to Plantation, Florida, communities across America have decided that they can no longer afford to continue growing as they have in the past. Seeking creative ways to manage growth, they have successfully gathered support for new visions of their communities and have seen their visions through to reality by enacting regulatory changes that led to on-the-ground new compact development.

This analysis attempts to provide some guidance to communities struggling with the same issues of accommodating new homes and businesses in a way that better uses existing land and infrastructure while creating exciting and memorable places that people love. A summary of the profiled communities follows; then, we analyze some key findings and principles drawn from the success of each community.

The following communities are profiled in this book (in ascending order from smallest to largest):

**Huntersville, North Carolina.** This commuter suburb of Charlotte has seen its population swell from 3,000 in 1990 to roughly 40,000 in 2007. With rapid growth came concerns about the way the community was developing. In 1996, Huntersville adopted a new zoning ordinance that sought to deter sprawl and incorporate traditional town-planning principles. The ordinance encourages new construction in urbanized areas and along transportation corridors while preserving rural and agricultural lands. The new regulations have led to the creation of successful new development that conforms to traditional design principles and creates a sense of place in an area that previously had seen only a typical sprawling development pattern.

**Evanston, Illinois.** A first-ring suburb of Chicago, Evanston has evolved into a more-diverse urban center to create a sense of place, making it competitive with suburban shopping centers and offices. Evanston has a population of 76,000 that is expanding because of new residential development downtown. By using higher densities, zoning changes, a special service district, two tax increment financing (TIF) districts, and a Planned Development Ordinance, the city was able to spur revitalization and redevelopment of downtown with higher-density compact development.

**Plantation, Florida.** Located ten miles (16.09 km) west of Fort Lauderdale, Plantation is home to 85,000 residents and growing. Anticipated population growth and land constraints (the Everglades to the west and the Atlantic Ocean to the east) have led Plantation and other communities in Broward County to conclude that growing up rather than out is the future of the region. In 2004, the city enacted new regulations that are transforming the Plantation Midtown District from a traditional suburban commercial district into a more-urban, walkable town center with a mix of uses and readily accessible public transportation.

**Ontario, California.** Located approximately 35 miles (56.33 km) east of downtown Los Angeles, the city of Ontario has seen significant residential and commercial development over the past two decades. With a growing population of 170,000 and a residential land use pattern that was traditionally low density, the city knew it had to make better use of the limited land remaining to better accommodate growth and leverage its investments in public infrastructure. In 1998, the city adopted the New Model Colony General Plan to guide the development of an 8,200-acre (3,318.42-hectare) tract of land. The goal of the plan is to create a diverse, walkable, compact mixed-use community with vibrant public space. New compact development has been constructed and buildout will take place over the next 30 years.

**Arlington County, Virginia (Columbia Pike).** Arlington County is nationally recognized for its exemplary planning efforts. With 202,800 residents, it is among the most densely populated jurisdictions in the United States. The county is known for planning higher-density nodes around its many Metro stops of the Washington, D.C., Metrorail system. The Columbia Pike corridor is not located along the Metro route and has suffered economically as a result. In 2003, after years of planning and visioning exercises, the county adopted the Columbia Pike Form-Based Code, which promotes the redevelopment of the corridor as a pedestrian-friendly higher-density community. Form-based codes focus on the shape of buildings and how they relate to each other and the street; the certainty of the codes creates less community opposition and allows expedited review.

**Seattle, Washington.** The population of Seattle is fast approaching 580,000 in a region of 3.3 million. The area has been attempting to reduce regional sprawl by encouraging more residential development in the city. A major part of this effort was significant changes to Seattle's downtown zoning code, which covers three downtown neighborhoods. The zoning code changes increase the floor/area ratio (FAR) and height for commercial buildings and the height for residential structures. In addition to the increased height, a 10 percent density bonus is offered if the developer contributes to affordable housing, child care, and civic or cultural projects such as open space and landmark theaters.

**Austin, Texas.** With a population of 735,000, the city of Austin is the center of a growing metropolitan area of 1.5 million. In 2004, the Austin City Council enacted the University Neighborhood Overlay (UNO), which applies to the West Campus neighborhood near the University of Texas campus. The UNO is an incentive-based zoning overlay that allows greater densities and encourages affordable housing. The overlay also provides design guidelines to create a positive streetscape and pedestrian experience. The new regulations allow the university to provide much-needed services and housing to its students while protecting the surrounding residential community.

**San Diego, California.** The city of San Diego covers 330 square miles (854.70 sq km) and has a population of more than 1.3 million. The city has seen explosive population growth for the past two decades, and projections call for continued growth, albeit slower than in the past. San Diego adopted the "City of Villages" (COV) growth strategy in 2002 as part of its update to the city's General Plan. The COV strategy encourages higher-density mixed-use villages in a pedestrian-friendly environment close to transit.

# Keys to Success

Although the profiles presented in this book represent a wide range of communities from across the country that vary in size from small to large, a series of consistent principles and lessons learned emerges. Other communities seeking to revise their regulations to encourage developers to respond to the growing market demand for more compact mixed-use development can view these principles and lessons learned as helpful guideposts from communities that have been through the process required to enact compact development regulations.

Before discussing the consistent principles that apply across all community types and sizes, we need to point out several significant differences and issues. First, the scope of the process of changing development regulations will differ. Large cities realistically cannot be expected to, nor would they want to, revise all their land use regulations to encourage compact development, whereas a small community could conceivably change its entire regulatory scheme at once.

A large city would more likely address one discrete district, a corridor, or sometimes one particular site at a time. In both large and small cities, the most effective method for change may be to set a general compact development *strategy* through some form of visioning and consensus-building exercises but then to work slowly through enacting the necessary regulatory changes needed to allow the private sector to respond to market demand for compact mixed-use development. A surgical approach of removing the biggest obstacles first and dealing with lesser obstacles over time may be most prudent and politically realistic.

Smaller communities may be able to revise all of their development regulations at one time. Such a process requires significant effort to address preservation of the existing community and to avoid unintended consequences of the newly enacted regulations. The goal of the effort is to strengthen the community through new compact development, redevelopment, and infill development without negatively affecting the existing community.

The fact that compact development is taking place on greenfield sites, on existing properties that are being redeveloped, and on infill sites highlights another difference. Regulations for infill development obviously address different issues and concerns from regulations for greenfield development (such as development in master-planned communities). Although developing each kind of site presents its own set of challenges, successful compact infill development requires increasing density of existing communities in a way that strengthens but does not disrupt established communities. Overseeing this type of increase in density is likely to be a trickier proposition than greenfield development or master-planned community development. With the supply of developable land diminishing in most metropolitan areas, compact infill development is likely to be more common than greenfield development. The two types of development present different challenges with a variety of potential solutions.

Another issue deserving discussion is the relationship between zoning, real estate market demand, and land values. Increasing the permitted density on specific parcels of land creates value. Some consideration should be given to how increasing the permitted density will increase property values, which, in turn, may affect the existing community. The higher land value will make redevelopment feasible. The loss of existing land uses caused by the increased development potential of the property should be anticipated. Preservation of cultural, historic, or architectural assets should be considered before making any regulatory change. Preserving existing affordable housing and planning for new housing that is affordable may be a concern, as well as preserving key parcels for public uses, such as schools and libraries. In addition, land values may possibly increase before enactment of any new development regulations solely because of speculation. The effect of this possibility may deserve some thought.

An understanding that market demand drives compact development highlights another important issue: rezoning a property for compact development may not lead to actual on-the-ground compact development if no market exists for that product. Understanding real estate market fundamentals can assist in aligning zoning and market demand. In too many communities, authorities assume that zoning for higher density will automatically lead to development of a new town center similar to that in a neighboring community. In reality, market demand will support only a given number of town centers, and professional market analysts may be needed to assess those possibilities. Therefore, communities should understand the reality of the limits of market demand when seeking to encourage new compact development.

Following are several principles and lessons learned that communities seeking to encourage and facilitate compact development through regulatory change may find helpful, although they should keep in mind the many differences that exist among the profiled communities.

**Do not overlook key stakeholders when creating a coalition of support.** Although the need to involve all stakeholders in the process of creating a coalition to support new compact development is hardly news, determining who the actual stakeholders are in a community can be more difficult than it seems. Several of the profiled communities reported being blindsided by unexpected opposition from groups they had inadvertently forgotten to include.

Early and broad stakeholder participation in creating a vision for a community and in designing a compact development strategy increases the

COURTESY OF ULI

Community charrettes and visioning workshops are critical tools for building consensus on compact development regulations.

likelihood of a smoother process later, when actual development proposals are submitted for community approval. Upfront visioning and planning can allow "by-right" development regulations that eliminate a variety of additional bureaucratic processes later, such as variances. Although including every potential stakeholder in the process and anticipating unanimous support are unrealistic, care should be taken to include stakeholders who have the ability to derail any plan or proposal after the work of the group is done. Key players that may be overlooked include representatives from local engineering, utility, and public works departments; environmental groups; building industry members; chambers of commerce; and housing advocacy groups.

Having the right coalition members can serve as a reality check for any proposal that might not be financially feasible or that might inaccurately gauge market demand or market fundamentals relating to the density required to support specific land uses. Issues of infrastructure capacity may likewise limit the scope of any proposal.

Many environmental groups understand and support compact development—specifically, mixed-use, infill, compact development that is connected to public transportation—as a solution to sprawl. Their support can be crucial to enactment; in contrast, leaving them out of the process can create a climate of distrust that can derail the efforts later in the process. Even if they agree with the broad outlines of the proposal, without trust, such groups may withhold vital public support.

Several of the profiled communities mentioned representation from the local public works department as a crucial component of the coalition-building process. Failure to include representation from agencies representing water, sewer, transportation, and other utilities can cause trouble down the road if infrastructure capacity is inadequate to support any new plan or proposal. In the same vein, developers and builders can provide feedback on whether the regulations will create the desired outcome or whether the market and the development community will ignore them—and why. Representation from the local financial community can provide similar feedback.

**Set the ground rules, and educate coalition members on anticipated population growth and real estate market fundamentals.** To create consensus on any vision, plan, or strategy for compact development among a diverse coalition of stakeholders with often polarized points of view, the stakeholders need to agree on some ground rules at the start. They also need to be educated on anticipated growth, as well as its impact on the community, and the real estate fundamentals that drive land development. The ground rules might include the following:
- The status quo is unacceptable.
- Growth will continue, and it is an indicator of a healthy community.

- Certain real estate market fundamentals drive land development.

Getting the group to agree that the status quo is unacceptable should not be too difficult because many people are unhappy with how their communities are growing and developing. The effects of continuing the status quo can be outlined. For a suburban market, the result may be the elimination of most open space for low-density development. For an urban market, it may lead to economic stagnation or decline caused by lack of new infill development or urban revitalization. This analysis sets a benchmark, lays out the consequences of inaction, and crystallizes the purpose of the process for the stakeholders in the coalition.

The most successful communities have demonstrated a firm grasp of the underlying market and financial forces that drive land development. Therefore, educating the coalition on real estate market fundamentals and anticipated population growth should be paramount at the start of the process.

An old planning expression goes, "there's only one thing worse than growth … and that's no growth." The sentiment of the expression is that although growth is painful, no growth signals the economic decline of a community, which has far worse implications. The whole purpose of comprehensive visioning and planning is to plan for that necessary growth. So laying out the challenge for stakeholders begins with laying out anticipated growth projections. The group needs to determine how these new residents will be accommodated—through new greenfield development, redevelopment of existing properties, infill development that strengthens rather than weakens the existing community, or a combination of these possibilities.

Last, educating members on density, housing types, requirements for retail and office development, and other real estate market fundamentals is important at the beginning to avoid unrealistic or inaccurate assumptions regarding land use and the real estate market. Fundamentals, such as the population density required to make public transportation viable, the number of rooftops required to support a grocery store or other retail uses, and the risks and costs associated with land development, should be understood. Without a firm grasp of real estate market fundamentals, stakeholders risk creating strategies, visions, or plans that bear no relation to market realities.

**Use deadlines to manage expectations and to keep the process moving forward.** As the case studies in this book demonstrate, the process of changing development regulations is time consuming but worthwhile. As mentioned earlier, the process will differ and time frames will vary depending upon the scope of the undertaking. Whether the goal is a strategy, vision, or plan for a single site or for an entire community, leaders of the process should allow a significant amount of time. The case studies demonstrate that to build the coalition of support (through adequate public meetings and input) that leads to some form of consensus will likely take a minimum of two years.

Although extended debate and delays should be anticipated, strict deadlines should be set and adhered to as much as is possible to avoid interminable debate. At some point, decisions must be made, and everyone involved in the process should know what that date is. The path toward completion of the regulatory change should be clear to all participants. The typical process may begin with community charrettes and visioning workshops, followed by fleshing out of the details of the vision and creation of some kind of community strategy, vision, or plan. The regulatory changes would then follow to implement the community strategy, vision, or plan. While ensuring that the public feels time for input has been adequate, each step in this process should have a deadline for completion.

**Reach a consensus on the strategy, vision, or plan before revising regulations.** Before crafting compact development regulations, all stakeholders should reach a consensus on a strategy, vision, or plan for the community, district, corridor, or site (depending on the scope of the project). Part of the process of reaching consensus can be testing different development scenarios. The analysis should assess the effects on outlying open space, the transportation network, government revenues and expenditures, and overall quality of life. After stakeholders agree on an overall strategy, vision, or plan for change, planning officials and elected and appointed leaders will begin the process of implementing the changes needed to support it. Without such a foundation, implementation efforts may encounter opposition and distrust among community members who might question the motives for the changes.

Consensus is defined as a state of general agreement within a group. Consensus does not mean complete agreement on every issue under consideration. Reaching consensus will be a process of compromise to reach a state of general agreement within the group. As mentioned earlier, setting and sticking to deadlines can force the group to reach consensus rather than seek unanimous agreement on every detail, which will likely be difficult—if not impossible.

In communities where environmental analysis is required, in some situations environmental analysis may be conducted concurrently with the consensus-building process so as not to delay a neighborhood's transformation. The lengthy process of environmental analysis can delay needed changes by a year or more, by which time the carefully constructed consensus may be lost.

**Remember that density is only a tool to help you build a great community.** Some of the most valuable and highly loved and respected places in the world are higher-density developments. For examples, think of all the great old urban neighborhoods in cities like Boston, New York, and San Francisco. These places are some of the most exclusive communities in the world—with astronomical property values. Likewise, some of the most despised and poorly constructed places are also higher density. For examples, think of the many public housing projects that were cheerfully imploded over the past few years. Many readers would be surprised to learn that the infamous Pruitt Igoe public housing project in St. Louis and Greenwich Village in New York City were equivalent in density. The point is that density is just one component of a place. The design of these places significantly affects how people feel about them. When people complain about density, often they are actually complaining about design. Density is but one tool for creating great places.

Nevertheless, appropriate density is required to make compact development work. Creating pedestrian- and bicycle-friendly compact development

requires increased densities. Low-density development simply does not create the efficiencies that compact development allows. Creating exciting, vibrant, efficient compact development through new greenfield development, redevelopment of underused sites, and infill development in exising neighborhoods requires density, but it is merely one means to an end.

Therefore, the focus of any visioning or planning process should be on building great communities and revitalizing established neighborhoods. The required densities to make the vision a reality are merely one important aspect needed to make the creation of the place possible. Various public transportation options, including light rail, buses, and trolleys, require a certain amount of population density within a certain distance to be financially viable. Retail uses, such as grocery stores, require threshold numbers of households within a certain distance to be viable. Too many communities want the retail and the mass transit without understanding the densities required to make both work.

**Building compactly around mass-transit stations can reduce reliance on automobiles and increase public transportation ridership.**

COURTESY OF ART CUETO, CREATIVE HOUSING ASSOCIATES

**Ensure that adequate infrastructure and sources of funding are available.** Integrating and coordinating the planning process for compact development with community planning for infrastructure investments is an important part of the comprehensive planning process. One of the strongest arguments for compact development is the efficiency that can be created by increasing densities and concentrating infrastructure investments in a less-dispersed area than is typical with low-density development. As such, having representation in any planning process from local departments such as public works, utilities, and engineering is important. In addition, funding sources for the infrastructure should be clearly outlined. If the development community is to pay for certain elements, that should be clearly outlined so development proposals can account for the additional expense in any assessment of financial feasibility of new compact development. In established communities, new development is often responsible for needed infrastructure improvements, often as mitigations required from the review process. An array of financing tools is available, including TIF, that can and should be considered in the process.

**Decide whether the market in your community will respond to incentive-based guidelines or required standards or a mix of the two.** In some markets, incentive-based development regulations work, perhaps because of a strong market or because the incentives are structured to make them financially feasible. In other markets, voluntary or incentive-based regulations might not bring about the outcome desired.

Those crafting new compact development regulations should attempt to follow the process a developer goes through when making a "go/no go" financial decision to determine whether the new regulations will make financial sense and whether developers will respond to incentive-based regulations. Poorly constructed regulations can often have unintended consequences. All possible efforts should be made to determine how the private sector development community will respond to the new regulations. Will developers ignore them? Will they develop elsewhere? Will they alter their development proposals to avoid them? The last is often the case in communities where regulations kick in at a certain development size (such as 50 residential units), causing a sudden proliferation of many 49-unit development proposals. In these cases, thinking like a developer (determining what incentive would lure the developer to comply and thereby achieve the desired result from the community's perspective) can be an effective technique for drafting successful regulation.

The University Neighborhood Overlay in Austin created an incentive-based system that tripled the allowable density in exchange for specific design and affordability requirements. This incentive has worked. The area has seen rapid development since enactment of the ordinance, and the regulations have created the type of community envisioned. By contrast, in Plantation, Florida, planners have found that voluntary regulations relating to a specific community concern have not provided adequate incentive and that mandatory regulations would have better ensured that their complete vision became reality.

**Strike the right balance between flexibility and certainty.** Although flexibility in compact development regulations can allow innovative projects, unclear and ambiguous regulations can lead to misunderstanding and development risk. Certainty in the development process can reduce risk; however, overly prescriptive and detailed regulations can stifle innovation. Striking the right balance between flexibility and certainty is the art of crafting effective regulations. Arlington County's form-based code provides a good example of creating specific requirements relating to the form of buildings while allowing flexibility in design, details, and uses.

**Pay close attention to the details, and visit completed compact development in other communities to visualize design concepts.** Getting density right means getting the details right. As densities increase, so does the importance of the details. Creating great places requires getting such elements as building height, sidewalk and street width, street size, and landscaping and parks to work together harmoniously to create memorable places that people enjoy. Everyone involved in the process of creating compact development regulations should become a full-time student of the built environment, noting places and spaces that work and analyzing why they work. Conversely (and perhaps of more importance), they should observe places and spaces that do not work, areas that make them feel uncomfortable or unsafe, and they should ask themselves what it is about the area that makes them feel that way. Determining how the relationships between the elements of design, including the uses and the users, work together will help ensure regulations that can achieve the community's goals.

Site visits with a tape measure can help quantify the specifics of places that just "feel right" and are thus very popular and well used. Great places are a collection of thousands of details that just work together well. In the continually evolving field of design, a variety of design solutions may be appropriate for a community. Design questions have no one answer, and issues such as architectural compatibility are contextual. Continual observation and feedback is important. Smaller communities may need to hire professional designers to help them.

**Provide design guidelines.** With such importance placed on details, design guidelines become increasingly important to the success of compact develop-

ment. The expression "a picture is worth a thousand words" applies to design guidelines and codes. Design guidelines illustrate the intent of the regulations and are often more effective in explaining the desired vision for the area than regulatory codes.

Most often, design guidelines that successfully encourage compact development are based on broad, substantive design principles. They should go beyond architectural elevations and sketches to articulate the intentions of compact design regulations—sustainability, community, and vibrancy. Broad, flexible design guidelines allow organic and creative design, whereas overly prescriptive standards can stifle innovation.

A coherent application of design guidelines at all stages of the development process is crucial to successful compact development. Too often, design standards are enforced unevenly or too late in the development process. Therefore, it is critical that the design expectations be addressed early and consistently throughout the course of development.

COURTESY OF TED WASHINGTON

**Appropriate density is critical in creating walkable, lively communities.**

Good design guidelines reconcile the relationship between the many components of private development, including the building and parking, with public spaces, such as streets and sidewalks. Getting such things right can make the difference between the success or failure of a development.

**Educate planning staff on compact development.** Several of the communities profiled had limited previous experience with compact development. Planning staff accustomed to dealing with single-use, low-density development will likely find new compact development proposals to be more complicated and more difficult to review and assess. A comprehensive education process for the entire planning department, from comprehensive planners to permit reviewers, should stress the importance of this new development type to the community.

In most communities, more mixed-use and higher-density development is the future as available land dwindles while population growth and job growth continue. Yet in many communities, the planning staff understands only what they have seen, which in many cases is low-density development that can be much less complex than compact development. With the complexity inherent in compact development becoming the norm, everyone involved in the public planning and entitlement process should be made aware that a new benchmark of skills is expected of them. This will be daunting to some but invigorating to others, who will view it as an opportunity to be in the forefront of the latest in planning and development. They should be given adequate tools and authority to facilitate this type of development.

**Adjust regulations as necessary.** Market conditions change, and regulations often have unintended consequences. For example, affordable housing requirements, if poorly constructed with little understanding of the actual housing market, can reduce housing supply and worsen the existing housing affordability problem. In addition, details are often missed when creating land use regulations. A hallmark of effective regulation is a system of regular assessment and revision. Several of the policies and programs highlighted in the community profiles in this publication have been revised, often more than once. If the goals of the community are not being met, assessing how the regulations could be revised to achieve community goals should be considered as important as the initial process of creating the regulation. Two of the profiled communities revised their regulations to address infrastructure costs. Another enacted revisions to address land preservation, and yet another amended its regulations several times to make some regulations mandatory rather than voluntary and to create design guidelines. Of course, the most effective way of assessing the success of the regulations is looking at the actual projects that resulted from the regulations. Were the actual outcomes those that were expected? Could the results have been better?

Revising land use regulations is not a failure of the initial regulations but rather a necessary part of the process. Real estate markets change rapidly; being responsive to such changes is a strength not a weakness.

1. Reid Ewing, Keith Bartholomew, Steve Winkelman, Jerry Walters, and Don Chen, *Growing Cooler: The Evidence on Urban Development and Climate Change* (Washington, DC: ULI, forthcoming 2008).

2. John K. McIlwain, "Point of View," *Multifamily Trends*, March/April 2008.

# Chapter 2

# Tools at a Glance

THE FOLLOWING TABLE PRESENTS POLICIES and tools used by localities and organizations across the country to encourage compact development. Also included in this table are the programs described in each of the case studies. Pertinent information on the program type, location, and implementation date of each resource as well as a brief description are arranged for easy access. For a more comprehensive account, each tool is referenced by page number and examined in greater detail later in the subsequent chapters.

# Tools at a Glance

## PROGRAM

| | LOCALITY/ORGANIZATION | STATE OR PROVINCE | FORM-BASED CODE | MODEL CODE | RESOURCE/PUBLICATION | MANDATORY PROGRAM | INCENTIVE PROGRAM | POPULATION OF LOCALITY | YEAR IMPLEMENTED/CREATED | PAGE NUMBER |
|---|---|---|---|---|---|---|---|---|---|---|
| **Case Studies** | | | | | | | | | | |
| **Huntersville Zoning Ordinance** Zoning changes adopted by jurisidiction to target compact development | Town of Huntersville | North Carolina | | | | ✓ | | 40,000 | 1996 | 32 |
| **Downtown Redevelopment, Evanston** Code crafted to encourage greater height and density in downtown area in return for design considerations | City of Evanston | Illinois | | | | | ✓ | 76,000 | 1993 | 39 |
| **Plantation Midtown District** New master plan and zoning district designed to encourage more dense, active mix of uses | City of Plantation | Florida | | | | ✓ | | 86,138 | 2002 | 47 |
| **New Model Colony General Plan** Mixed-use plan designed to encompass a mix of uses connected through a network of greenways and open space | City of Ontario | California | | | | ✓ | | 170,000 | 1998 | 57 |
| **Columbia Pike Form-Based Code** Voluntary form-based code designed to encourage mixed uses and economic development along an automobile-congested commercial street | County of Arlington | Virginia | ✓ | | | | ✓ | 202,800 | 2002 | 67 |
| **Downtown Zoning Changes** Revisions to the downtown zoning code allowed dramatically higher densities in hopes of curbing sprawl | City of Seattle | Washington | | | | | ✓ | 580,000 | 2006 | 74 |
| **University Neighborhood Overlay** Incentive-based overlay district permits greater densities in exchange for streetscape improvements | City of Austin | Texas | | | | | ✓ | 735,000 | 2004 | 88 |
| **City of Villages** Planning strategy designed to create mixed-use villages close to mass transit | City of San Diego | California | | | | ✓ | | 1,300,000 | 2004 | 94 |

# Tools at a Glance

## PROGRAM

| PROGRAM | LOCALITY/ORGANIZATION | STATE OR PROVINCE | FORM-BASED CODE | MODEL CODE | RESOURCE/PUBLICATION | MANDATORY PROGRAM | INCENTIVE PROGRAM | POPULATION OF LOCALITY | YEAR IMPLEMENTED/CREATED | PAGE NUMBER |
|---|---|---|---|---|---|---|---|---|---|---|
| **Codes** | | | | | | | | | | |
| **Central Petaluma Specific Plan** Form-based code that replaced conventional zoning for city; guides architectural and urban design | City of Petaluma | California | ✓ | | | | ✓ | 54,660 | 2003 | 105 |
| **Fort Worth's Mixed-Use Zoning Standards** Designates mixed-use growth centers and urban villages | City Fort Worth | Texas | ✓ | | | | ✓ | 653,320 | 2005 | 105 |
| **Form-Based Codes: Implementing Smart Growth** Illustrated guide to adopting form-based codes | Local Government Commission | | | | ✓ | | | | 2004 | 105 |
| **SmartCode** Unified land development ordinance that includes zoning, subdivision regulations, urban design, and architectural standards | Duany Plater-Zyberk/ PlaceMakers | | ✓ | ✓ | ✓ | | | | 2003 | 105 |
| **Smart Neighborhoods** Model ordinance for mixed-use and compact design overlay zones | State of Maryland | Maryland | | ✓ | ✓ | | | | 2001 | 106 |
| **Models and Guidelines for Infill Development** Rural, suburban, and urban strategies for infill development | State of Maryland | Maryland | | ✓ | ✓ | | | | 2001 | 106 |
| **Model Ordinances for Sustainable Development** Model ordinances to help local communities implement sustainable development | State of Minnesota | Minnesota | | ✓ | | | | | 2000 | 106 |
| **Model Zoning Technical Advisory Group** Report on methods to simplify process and reduce cost of compact development at the local and state levels | State of Minnesota | Minnesota | | | ✓ | | | | 2003 | 106 |

# Tools at a Glance

## PROGRAM

| PROGRAM | LOCALITY/ORGANIZATION | STATE OR PROVINCE | FORM-BASED CODE | MODEL CODE | RESOURCE/PUBLICATION | MANDATORY PROGRAM | INCENTIVE PROGRAM | POPULATION OF LOCALITY | YEAR IMPLEMENTED/CREATED | PAGE NUMBER |
|---|---|---|---|---|---|---|---|---|---|---|
| **Alternatives to Conventional Zoning Project** Model codes offering a variety of alternative zoning approaches to Georgia's local governments | State of Georgia | Georgia | | ✓ | | | | | 2002 | 106 |
| **Commercial and Mixed-Use Code Development Handbook** Strategies, best practices, and model ordinances for smart development | State of Oregon | Oregon | | ✓ | ✓ | | | | 1999 | 107 |
| **Infill and Redevelopment Code Handbook** Tools to encourage infill and redevelopment in urban areas | State of Oregon | Oregon | | ✓ | ✓ | | | | 1999 | 107 |
| **Model Development Code and User's Guide for Small Cities** Alternative zoning codes tailored to the needs of smaller towns and cities | State of Oregon | Oregon | | ✓ | ✓ | | | | 2005 | 107 |
| **Unraveling the Mysteries of Code Writing** Article detailing a five-step process for code revision | American Planning Association | | | | ✓ | | | | 2003 | 107 |
| **Smart Growth Zoning Codes: A Resource Guide** Examples of 150 smart growth ordinances from around the country that support smart growth objectives | Local Government Commission | | | ✓ | ✓ | | | | 2003 | 108 |
| **Model Smart Land Development Regulations** Comprehensive model smart growth codes | American Planning Association | | | ✓ | | | | | 2006 | 108 |

# Tools at a Glance

## PROGRAM

| PROGRAM | LOCALITY/ORGANIZATION | STATE OR PROVINCE | FORM-BASED CODE | MODEL CODE | RESOURCE/PUBLICATION | MANDATORY PROGRAM | INCENTIVE PROGRAM | POPULATION OF LOCALITY | YEAR IMPLEMENTED/CREATED | PAGE NUMBER |
|---|---|---|---|---|---|---|---|---|---|---|
| **LEED for Neighborhood Development** National rating system for neighborhood design that incorporates the principles of smart growth, urbanism, and green building | U.S. Green Building Council | | | | ✓ | | | | 2007 | 108 |
| **New Jersey Rehabilitation Subcode** Flexible rehabilitation subcode for renovations and rehabilitation of existing structures | State of New Jersey | New Jersey | ✓ | | | ✓ | | | 1998 | 109 |
| **Building Rehabilitation Code Program** Rehabilitation code for existing buildings intended to streamline renovation process | State of Maryland | Maryland | ✓ | | | ✓ | | | 2001 | 109 |
| **Nationally Applicable Recommended Rehabilitation Provisions** Provisions developed to guide regulation of repairs, rehabilitation, and reconstruction of existing structures | United States Department of Housing and Urban Development | | | ✓ | ✓ | | | | 1997 | 110 |
| **Smart Codes: Smart Growth Tools for Main Street** Overview of progressive rehabilitation codes adopted by various states and municipalities and municipalities | National Trust for Historic Preservation | | | | ✓ | | | | 2001 | 110 |
| **Zoning** | | | | | | | | | | |
| **Plantation Midtown District** New master plan and zoning district designed to encourage more dense, active mix of uses | City of Plantation | Florida | | | | | ✓ | 86,138 | 2002 | 112 |
| **Mixed-Use Zoning Districts** Nine mixed-use districts designed to reflect unique characteristics of each area | City of Albany | Oregon | | | | | ✓ | 42,280 | 2007 | 112 |

## Tools at a Glance

### PROGRAM

| PROGRAM | LOCALITY/ORGANIZATION | STATE OR PROVINCE | FORM-BASED CODE | MODEL CODE | RESOURCE/PUBLICATION | MANDATORY PROGRAM | INCENTIVE PROGRAM | POPULATION OF LOCALITY | YEAR IMPLEMENTED/CREATED | PAGE NUMBER |
|---|---|---|---|---|---|---|---|---|---|---|
| **Highlands Garden Village**<br>Case study of 27-acre compact, mixed-use Planned Unit Development | City of Denver | Colorado | | | ✓ | | | | 1998 | 113 |
| **A Guide to Planned Unit Development**<br>Guide for local goverments on using PUDs to add flexibility and density to their zoning codes | State of New York | New York | | | ✓ | | | | 2005 | 113 |
| **Mixed-Use Overlay Zone**<br>Mixed-use overlay aimed at encouraging market-driven, mixed-use development and higher-density residential projects | City of Anaheim | Califorina | | | | ✓ | | 345,556 | 2004 | 114 |
| **Compact Development Overlay Zone**<br>Overlay zone designed to encourage higher-density residential uses within the urban growth boundary | City of Salem | Oregon | | | | | ✓ | 152,290 | 2002 | 114 |
| **Smart Neighborhoods**<br>Model overlay district ordinance designed to help local governments encourage mixed-use and compact development within the framework of conventional zoning | State of Maryland | Maryland | ✓ | | | | | | 1997 | 114 |
| **Development Types** | | | | | | | | | | |
| **Land Recycling Program**<br>Program designed to overcome the impediments to voluntary cleanup and reuse of brownfields | Commonwealth of Pennsylvania | Pennsyl-vania | | | | | ✓ | | 1995 | 116 |
| **Washington's Landing**<br>Case study of a successful public/private partnership that converted a brownfield into a mixed-use development | City of Pittsburgh | Pennsyl-vania | | | ✓ | | | | 1987 | 116 |

## Tools at a Glance

### PROGRAM

| PROGRAM | LOCALITY/ORGANIZATION | STATE OR PROVINCE | FORM-BASED CODE | MODEL CODE | RESOURCE/PUBLICATION | MANDATORY PROGRAM | INCENTIVE PROGRAM | POPULATION OF LOCALITY | YEAR IMPLEMENTED/CREATED | PAGE NUMBER |
|---|---|---|---|---|---|---|---|---|---|---|
| **Brownfields and Housing: How Are State VCPs Encouraging Residential Development?** Survey conducted to examine the potential of converting brownfields to residential development | Northeast-Midwest Institute | | | | ✓ | | | | 2000 | 117 |
| **Model Zoning Ordinance for Rural Cluster Development** Model ordinance that mandates cluster design within the district boundaries, ensuring large tracts of open space | Southeastern Wisconsin Regional Planning Commission | Wisconsin | ✓ | | | | | | 2002 | 118 |
| **Massachusetts Conservation Subdivision Design Project** Educational tools, model ordinances, and case studies created to overcome negative perception of cluster development | Boston Metropolitan Area Planning Council | Massa-chusetts | ✓ | ✓ | | | | | 2000 | 118 |
| **Conservation Design Books** Publications on the use of local ordinances and codes to promote conservation design | Greener Prospects | | | | ✓ | | | | 1996, 1999 | 118 |
| **Regulatory Strategies for Encouraging Infill and Redevelopment** Guide designed to assist local governments in implementing strategies for infill development within their communities | City of Denver | Colorado | | | ✓ | | | | 2006 | 119 |
| **Model Subdivision Regulations** Model regulations for localities seeking to incorporate smart growth principles in their codes | Southern Maine Regional Planning Commission | Maine | ✓ | | | | | | 1996 | 120 |

# Tools at a Glance

## PROGRAM

| PROGRAM | LOCALITY/ORGANIZATION | STATE OR PROVINCE | FORM-BASED CODE | MODEL CODE | RESOURCE/PUBLICATION | MANDATORY PROGRAM | INCENTIVE PROGRAM | POPULATION OF LOCALITY | YEAR IMPLEMENTED/CREATED | PAGE NUMBER |
|---|---|---|---|---|---|---|---|---|---|---|
| **Southside Neighborhood Redevelopment** Example of mixed-use, infill project that was assisted by the creation of a Traditional Neighborhood District ordinance | City of Greensboro | North Carolina | | | ✓ | | | 244,610 | 1995 | 120 |
| **Traditional Neighborhood District Ordinance** State legislation requiring all cities and villages over 12,500 in population to adopt a TND ordinance by 2010 | State of Wisconsin | Wisconsin | | | | ✓ | | | 1999 | 121 |
| **Comprehensive Program on Transit-Supportive Land Use** Overlay zones aimed at encouraging transit-oriented development around proposed stations in anticipation of 2008 light-rail system | City of Phoenix | Arizona | | | | | ✓ | 1,512,986 | 2004 | 122 |
| **Transit Village Initiative** Incentive program aimed at encouraging residential and retail development around existing transit facilities | New Jersey Department of Transportation | New Jersey | | | | | ✓ | | 1999 | 123 |
| **Transit District Development Plan** General TOD strategy to encourage development of compact, mixed-use neighborhoods near transit station | City of West Hyattsville | Maryland | | | | | ✓ | 14,733 | 1998 | 123 |
| **Transit-Oriented Development Code** TOD ordinance adopted by jurisidiction in anticipation of light-rail transit system | Town of Huntersville | North Carolina | | | | ✓ | | 40,000 | 1996 | 123 |
| **Transit Station Communities Project** Program designed to promote TOD throughout the Puget Sound area | City of Seattle | Washington | | | | | ✓ | 580,000 | 2000 | 124 |

# Tools at a Glance

## PROGRAM

| PROGRAM | LOCALITY/ORGANIZATION | STATE OR PROVINCE | FORM-BASED CODE | MODEL CODE | RESOURCE/PUBLICATION | MANDATORY PROGRAM | INCENTIVE PROGRAM | POPULATION OF LOCALITY | YEAR IMPLEMENTED/CREATED | PAGE NUMBER |
|---|---|---|---|---|---|---|---|---|---|---|
| **TOD Overlay** Incentive-based TOD overlay district designed to encourage property owners to apply compact development principles near mass transit | City of Salt Lake City | Utah | | | | | ✓ | 178,858 | 2006 | 124 |
| **Rosslyn-Ballston Corridor** General Land Use Plan requiring compact, mixed-use development around county's Metro stations, resulting in active urban transit villages | County of Arlington | Virginia | | | | ✓ | | 202,800 | 1996 | 124 |
| **Central City Transportation Management Plan** Plan promotes mixed-use and higher-density development to reduce regional vehicular use | City of Portland | Oregon | | | | | ✓ | 537,081 | 1995 | 124 |
| **Transit-Oriented Design Manual** Design manual provides visual examples of desired transit-oriented development | City of Burlington | Vermont | | | | ✓ | | 38,889 | 2002 | 124 |
| **Density and Design Tools** | | | | | | | | | | |
| **Accessory Dwelling Unit Development Program** Program designed to encourage and educate homeowners on the conversion and construction of accessory dwelling units | City of Santa Cruz | California | | | | | ✓ | 54,593 | 2003 | 126 |
| **Small Lot Subdivision Ordinance** Ordinance streamlines subdivision and entitlement process to encourage infill development | City of Los Angeles | California | | | | | ✓ | 3,800,000 | 2005 | 126 |
| **Model State Act and Local Ordinance** Report including model state and local ordinances for accessory dwelling units | AARP/American Planning Association | | | ✓ | | | | | 2000 | 126 |
| **Northpoint** Case study on 45-acre mixed-use infill project developed under design guidelines | City of Cambridge | Massa-chusetts | | | ✓ | | | | 2005 | 127 |

## Tools at a Glance

| PROGRAM | LOCALITY/ORGANIZATION | STATE OR PROVINCE | FORM-BASED CODE | MODEL CODE | RESOURCE/PUBLICATION | MANDATORY PROGRAM | INCENTIVE PROGRAM | POPULATION OF LOCALITY | YEAR IMPLEMENTED/CREATED | PAGE NUMBER |
|---|---|---|---|---|---|---|---|---|---|---|
| **Great American Neighborhood: Contemporary Design Principles for Building Livable Residential Communities** <br> Report outlining design principles that can be used to create traditional neighborhoods that appeal to market demands | Maine State Planning Office/ GrowSmart Maine | Maine | | | ✓ | | | | 2004 | 127 |
| **Fort Collins Design Manual** <br> Illustrated design manual that encourages compact development | City of Fort Collins | Colorado | | | | ✓ | | 630,000 | 2000 | 127 |
| **Design Review Manual** <br> A guide to developing an architectural assessment ordinance in historic communities | Blackstone River Valley | Massa- chusetts Rhode Island | | | ✓ | | | | 2003 | 128 |
| **Development Design Handbook** <br> Handbook highlighting a flexible development design process that incorporates elements of compact development | City of Salem | Oregon | | | | ✓ | | 152,290 | 2006 | 128 |
| **Smart Growth Policy Document** <br> Incentivized smart growth guidelines that encourage higher-density, pedestrian-friendly redevelopment | City of Mobile | Alabama | | | ✓ | | ✓ | 198,915 | 2003 | 129 |
| **Compact Development Endorsement Program** <br> Endorsement program that encourages compact development and streamlines development process | San Francisco Greenbelt Alliance | California | | | | | ✓ | | 1999 | 129 |
| **Smart Growth Scorecard** <br> Scorecard that evaluates smart growth features for statewide projects | State of Maryland | Maryland | | | ✓ | | | | 1997 | 130 |

# Tools at a Glance

## PROGRAM

| PROGRAM | LOCALITY/ORGANIZATION | STATE OR PROVINCE | FORM-BASED CODE | MODEL CODE | RESOURCE/PUBLICATION | MANDATORY PROGRAM | INCENTIVE PROGRAM | POPULATION OF LOCALITY | YEAR IMPLEMENTED/CREATED | PAGE NUMBER |
|---|---|---|---|---|---|---|---|---|---|---|
| **Smart Growth Scorecard** Two scorecards designed to rate private development and municipalities on smart growth criteria | New Jersey Future | New Jersey | | | ✓ | | | | 2002 | 130 |
| **Home Development Endorsement Criteria** Business association that developed endorsement criteria to support residential proposals discouraging sprawl | Silicon Valley Leadership Group | California | | | | | ✓ | | 1977 | 130 |
| **Housing Endorsement Program** Endorsement program that seeks to encourage residential development based on smart growth principles | Vermont Smart Growth Collaborative | Vermont | | | ✓ | | | | 2001 | 131 |
| **TOD Incentive Program** Countywide TOD incentive program to encourage local land use authorities to develop housing near transit stations | County of San Mateo | California | | | | | ✓ | 712,462 | 1999 | 132 |
| **Housing Incentive Program** Metropolitan Transportation Commission that allocates regional transportation funds to encourage TOD | City of San Francisco | California | | | | | ✓ | 744,041 | 2000 | 132 |
| **Livable Centers Initiative** Program that awards grants to local governments and nonprofits to support linkage of transportation and land use | Atlanta Regional Commission | Georgia | | | | | ✓ | 3,925,400 | 1999 | 132 |
| **Livable Communities Act** Voluntary, incentive-based grant program designed to support connected development patterns and affordable housing | Minneapolis-St. Paul | Minnesota | | | | | ✓ | 3,500,000 | 1995 | 133 |

## Tools at a Glance

### PROGRAM

| PROGRAM | LOCALITY/ORGANIZATION | STATE OR PROVINCE | FORM-BASED CODE | MODEL CODE | RESOURCE/PUBLICATION | MANDATORY PROGRAM | INCENTIVE PROGRAM | POPULATION OF LOCALITY | YEAR IMPLEMENTED/CREATED | PAGE NUMBER |
|---|---|---|---|---|---|---|---|---|---|---|
| **Smart Growth Overlay** State law that allows localities to provide incentives and technical assistance for development within smart growth overlay districts | Massachusetts Department of Housing and Community Development | Massa-chusetts | | | | | ✓ | | 2005 | 133 |
| **Community and Transportation Linkage Planning Program** Linkage program providing communities with technical support for local transportation planning efforts | City of Albany | New York | | | | | ✓ | 93,963 | 2000 | 134 |
| **TDM Encyclopedia** Regularly updated, comprehensive TDM encyclopedia that includes a variety of strategies, policies, and resources | Victoria Transport Policy Institute | British Columbia | | | ✓ | | | | 2007 | 135 |
| **TDM Policy** County requirement that all developers seeking site plan approval complete a Transportation Demand Management Plan | County of Arlington | Virginia | | | | ✓ | | 202,800 | 1990 | 135 |
| **Planning and Visioning** | | | | | | | | | | |
| **Community Visioning Workshop** Visioning process among city stakeholders that resulted in modified zoning, architectural design review process, and shared parking | Town of Suffield | Connecticut | | | ✓ | | | 13,552 | 2006 | 139 |
| **Visioning and Facilitation Services** Technical assistance and resource program designed to encourage local visioning efforts statewide | Florida Department of Community Affairs | Florida | | | ✓ | | | | 2000 | 139 |

## Tools at a Glance

| PROGRAM | LOCALITY/ORGANIZATION | STATE OR PROVINCE | FORM-BASED CODE | MODEL CODE | RESOURCE/PUBLICATION | MANDATORY PROGRAM | INCENTIVE PROGRAM | POPULATION OF LOCALITY | YEAR IMPLEMENTED/CREATED | PAGE NUMBER |
|---|---|---|---|---|---|---|---|---|---|---|
| **Urban Design Studio** Organization that provides technical assistance and charrettes for local communities on transportation and land use planning issues | Florida Treasure Coast Regional Planning Council | Florida | | | ✓ | | | | 1989 | 139 |
| **Reality Check Guide** Regional visioning program designed to engage regional leaders in dialogue on growth issues | Urban Land Institute | | | | ✓ | | | | 2005 | 140 |
| **Community Charrette** Result of weeklong charrette devoted to addressing transportation and land use issues in rural Wyoming county | County of Teton | Wyoming | | | ✓ | | 18,251 | | 2001 | 140 |
| **Visualizing Density** Essay and illustrated manual on planning and designing "good" density | Lincoln Institute of Land Policy | | | | ✓ | | | | 2007 | 140 |
| **Image Library** Comprehensive image library of of bicycle-and pedestrian-friendly environments | Pedestrian and Bicycle Information Center | | | | ✓ | | | | 1999 | 140 |
| **Neighborhood Explorations: This View of Density** Density calculator with images that illustrate various land use patterns and their effects on transportation and the environment | San Francisco League of Conservative Voters | | | | ✓ | | | | 2004 | 140 |
| **CommunityViz Software** GIS software designed to help communities visualize, analyze, and communicate about important land use scenarios | CommunityViz | | | | ✓ | | | | 2001 | 140 |
| **Miami 21 Plan** Transect-based planning approach designed to replace the traditional zoning code of the city | City of Miami | Florida | ✓ | | | | 404,048 | | 2007 | 141 |

# Chapter 3

# Community Case Studies

Huntersville Zoning Ordinance, Huntersville, North Carolina

Downtown Redevelopment, Evanston, Illinois

Plantation Midtown District, Plantation, Florida

New Model Colony, Ontario, California

Columbia Pike Form-Based Code, Arlington County, Virginia

Downtown Zoning Changes, Seattle, Washington

University Neighborhood Overlay, Austin, Texas

City of Villages, San Diego, California

# Huntersville Zoning Ordinance, Huntersville, North Carolina

Concerns about rapid growth prompted the town of Huntersville to adopt new zoning ordinances in November 1996 that sought to deter sprawl and incorporate "traditional town planning principles" to guide development. The principles include street connectivity, concentration of higher-density development along transportation corridors, transit-oriented residential development, and design that emphasizes community character.

*For more information:*

Huntersville Town Planning Philosophy and
    Zoning Ordinance Highlights
http://www.Huntersville.org/planning_1.asp

*Contact information:*

Jack Simoneau
Planning Director
Town of Huntersville
704-875-7000
jsimoneau@Huntersville.org

## Community Information

The town of Huntersville is located 15 miles (24.14 km) north of Charlotte, North Carolina, in Mecklenburg County. Along with nearby Cornelius and Davidson, it makes up the area known as "North Meck." Many residents are commuters to downtown Charlotte with easy access via Interstate 77 and express bus transportation.

In addition, nearby Lake Norman is a major recreational attraction for boaters and water skiers. The large artificial lake was created to serve the region's electrical needs.

Huntersville was primarily a rural, agricultural community with a small, relatively stable population through the late 1980s. However, since 1990—when the population of the town was a mere 3,000—Huntersville has experienced skyrocketing growth. As of 2007, approximately 40,000 people live there because the greater Charlotte area has mushroomed and newcomers are attracted to Huntersville by lower housing costs and recreational opportunities.

## Community Government Structure

Like most cities and counties in North Carolina, the town of Huntersville has a council manager form of government. Residents elect the mayor and board of commissioners, who then appoint a professional town manager to oversee daily municipal operations. The town of Huntersville has a mayor and a five-member board of commissioners. The town also has

Plans for the civic core of Huntersville include a town plaza, an open-air market, and a light-rail station.

COURTESY OF THE LAWRENCE GROUP

Citizens and public officials collaborate at a public design charrette for the Huntersville Downtown Master Plan.

COURTESY OF THE LAWRENCE GROUP

an appointed planning board to advise the town board on land use planning and zoning and a board of adjustments to consider zoning variances.

The planning department works with Huntersville's elected and appointed officials as well as the public to identify and implement long-range visions for the town's future and to enforce ordinances and regulations created to fulfill the long-term plan, such as those related to urban design, transportation, and environmental standards.

## Policy Enactment

Historically a small, slow-growing town, Huntersville began to experience growth pressures from the nearby greater Charlotte metropolitan area in the early 1990s that threatened to transform the community with suburban sprawl. Local residents, concerned about losing the town's distinctive identity, sought to take a strategic approach. From 1994 to 1995, the town mayor and council members initiated the development of a community vision and land use plan for Huntersville in an effort to define and maintain its rural, small-town character. While in the process of producing new regulations to implement the community's vision, the town adopted a one-year moratorium on new construction. This move helped discourage a rush on building permit requests before anticipated changes in regulations and freed up the two-person staff of the planning office to dedicate their time to the comprehensive planning effort.

The process began with informal conversations in the small community (which had a population of about 8,000 at the time) and the distribution of published materials to promote the planning process. The town council appointed a steering

committee to lead the effort to develop a vision for the future of Huntersville, work with the planning department, and structure a planning process and publicity strategy to get community input. In a series of three open houses in 1995, about 120 participants took part in a visual appearance survey that encouraged viewers to compare preferences for suburban strip development with compact, mixed-use streetscapes in residential, commercial, and retail settings. In these workshops, 98 percent of the participants expressed a preference for more traditional, walkable forms of town development with generous public spaces.

In fall 1996, the Charlotte Real Estate and Building Industry Coalition organized some reaction against the effort. However, local political leadership was committed to a plan that reflected the community preferences for traditional neighborhood development, and their commitment helped overcome possible objections. To assist with the production of a townwide mandatory code, Huntersville engaged urban design professor David Walters of the University of North Carolina–Charlotte College of Architecture to work with the town planning director and the steering committee.

At the end of 1996, the Huntersville town commissioners approved the new, mandatory zoning code to completely replace the former zoning code. The new code encourages new construction in the town's urbanized areas and along existing and proposed transportation corridors to the north and south, while preserving open space in more-rural areas to the east and west. The zoning code applies new urbanist principles in "Traditional Neighborhood Design" (TND) districts. These principles include an emphasis on public spaces, street and building design, and connectivity for pedestrians. In 2003, the zoning code was modified to reflect changes that would more strongly define and support appropriate development to preserve rural character in applicable areas.

After the code's adoption, the development community explored how to meet the new code. The biggest complaint involved the need to redo housing plans to accommodate the design requirements—such as restrictions on front-loading garages—which had to be significantly recessed or accessed from the back of the lot.

## Policy Details

The Huntersville development code promotes compact development in already developed areas supported by existing infrastructure, as well as clustered development in more-rural areas sited to encourage open-space preservation and preserve local landscapes. The development code also seeks to encourage a pattern of land uses that will support proposed future transit service between the towns of North Mecklenburg and the city of Charlotte, particularly higher-density housing within a five-minute walk of transit stations.

Some of the highlights of the zoning code include the following:

**Design features:** Build-to lines (rather than setback lines) are established that move structures closer to the street in urbanized areas, and larger setbacks buffered by street trees are allowed in less-urban settings. Parking lots are not permitted in the frontyard and must be located on the side or rear of buildings. In fact, parking or unattractive uses are screened.

Building scale and design compatibility with existing building design are emphasized, with particular attention to human scale and pedestrian entrances. In limited cases where buildings are not in proportion to human scale, large buffers are required. A mix of uses is encouraged.

**Density:** In the more urbanized areas near the interstate and proposed rail-transit line, Neighborhood Residential (NR) is the predomi-

The town's mandatory zoning code concentrates new construction along existing transit routes, preserving open space and rural areas.

nant zoning district. The NR zone has no density, lot size, or lot-width limits. Subdivisions approved in this zone range in density from 1.75 to 4.5 units an acre for single-family homes and up to 8 units per acre for multifamily units. In residential developments within one-quarter to one-half mile (0.4 to 0.8 km) of proposed rail transit stops, a transit-oriented development and residential zoning district may be applied for where a minimum density of 15 units an acre is required.

**Connectivity:** Multimodal access to streets for pedestrians and cyclists as well as the efficient distribution of traffic and lower speeds on city streets are promoted. Culs-de-sac are discouraged and may be used only where topography or lot layouts offer no other practical alternatives for connections.

**Mix of uses:** Mixed-use districts allow buildings of different uses but a similar design type to be sited in proximity to each other and encourage pedestrian access to local retail.

**Mixed-income/affordability:** Residential districts support a mix of housing types and lot sizes, which is intended to also encourage a wider range of price points. Up to 30 percent of housing units in a major subdivision may be multifamily units by right, and single-family homes are permitted to have accessory dwellings. Infill lots are allowed to have apartments or attached units by right.

**Open space/parks:** New developments are emphasized in urbanized areas that include public spaces, such as squares, greens, parks, or plazas, to enhance civic life and recreation located within one-quarter mile (0.4 km) of each lot. The regulations and zoning code, however, seek to delineate clear edges between town and country. Rural areas may have new developments, but these should be sited to preserve natural landscapes.

**Conditional zoning:** The town created parallel conditional zones for each zoning district estab-

COURTESY OF THE LAWRENCE GROUP

The Huntersville Town Center is planned for dense, mixed-use development with street-level retail and restaurants below office and residential uses.

lished. The conditional zoning district allows the developer to be specific about how it intends to develop the property if rezoned so that citizens and elected officials know what to expect. Developers can be as specific or as general as they want on the level of detail provided. However, the more specific rezoning development plans are, the less likely are future surprises. Most new rezoning requests are filed as conditional rezonings.

By and large, the public has favorably received the Huntersville zoning code and projects built under it, particularly in urbanized areas with compact traditional neighborhood development. The changes in the code have called more attention to design details, improved connectivity, and stimulated a closer examination of the relationship between proposed developments and surrounding development as well as the town as a whole. As new mixed-use projects are proposed, developments such as Birkdale Village, Rosedale, and Vermillion serve as real-life examples of successful projects.

Homebuilders have learned how to reformulate their standard designs to meet Huntersville's requirements and have found receptive markets for their efforts. The 2003 code amendments reaffirmed the town's confidence in the majority of the regulations adopted in 1996, particularly those that were relevant to the town's urbanized areas. The notable changes were primarily to support the preservation of open space and to guide development in rural parts of the town.

## Lessons Learned

The commitment of town leadership to reformulating the town's zoning code and regulations to achieve the community vision for the future was key to the success of Huntersville's effort to reshape its development patterns. This commitment helped create a community vision for the future and get the completely revamped land use policy and regulations in place to support that vision in only 18 months. Later review of the policy in 2003 allowed certain revisions for open-space and rural development.

**Start with developing a common vision.** The appointed steering committee led the way for Huntersville to identify and create a community-based vision for the future, which became a vital strategic foundation for the new zoning code and land use regulations.

**Establish a firm deadline and adhere to it.** In an attempt to achieve universal consensus, a regulatory reform project may be extended over many years. However, such lengthy negotiations tend to dilute the result and fail to implement the community's vision. Huntersville's one-year moratorium on development and 18-month total turnaround time made for a very efficient process.

**Focus on design over density.** The community was able to adopt the new zoning code with a focus on design standards, rather than density requirements—even though in many cases, the end product for urbanized areas did achieve a higher density of units.

**Clarify that TND is being applied selectively.** Despite the popular appeal of the concept of "traditional neighborhood design"—and the marketing of a variety of projects in Huntersville as such, sometimes inaccurately—in fact, not all of the town's zoning code is crafted to produce TND development. Rather, the regulations sought to improve subdivision design overall, with selected areas approved for TND districts that qualify as true traditional neighborhood design with a mix of uses, public spaces, and multimodal access.

**Provide a design book.** Although the zoning ordinance is well illustrated with examples of street design and layout of public spaces, no architectural design book existed to provide guidance to builders who faced the prospect of reconfiguring their housing designs to meet the new regulations. While some builders created design books independently to secure approval for compliance, initially developments suffered from a limited number of housing plans and too much repetition.

**Review built projects for desired outcomes, and adjust regulations if needed.** As projects have been completed under the new code, the town needed to look critically at the results to see if they met expectations. For instance, some of the alleys installed early on were too narrow to accommodate service vehicles. Furthermore, the intensity of development in the more-rural areas of the town's zoning jurisdiction did not fit with the character of the surrounding community and was the subject of 2003 amendments to the code.

## Featured Development: Birkdale Village

Birkdale Village was the first large-scale, mixed-use development to be built in a traditional neighborhood district under Huntersville's new zoning code. The site, formerly farmland, is located close to major transportation corridors that include Sam Furr Road/NC 73 to the east and west, and Interstate 77 to the north and south. Completed in 2002, the development is a 52-acre (21-hectare), pedestrian-oriented, mixed-use project with 287,000 square feet (26,663.17 square meters) of office and retail space and 320 one- to three-bedroom apartments (six units per acre).

The main street is built on a traditional grid system at a pedestrian scale with residential and mixed-use buildings; parking decks are located behind the buildings. On-street parking is available in parallel and angled spaces. Designed in the style of a Nantucket village with siding exteriors and high, sloping roofs, the two- to four-story buildings along the main street have ground-floor retail and rental apartments above. Most of the apartments (81 percent) are located above the retail space.

Retail tenants include several major national chains, such as Barnes & Noble, Banana Republic, Gap, Williams-Sonoma, Talbots, Ann Taylor, Victoria's Secret, Pier One, and Dick's Sporting Goods, as well as a variety of local retailers. Eastern Federal's 16-screen Movies at Birkdale theater was one of the first tenants to open on the site. The property also includes 11 eateries that range in offerings from fine dining to wine bars, ice cream parlors, and coffee shops.

Public spaces punctuate Birkdale Village frequently, providing numerous recreational and community gathering spaces. They include a linear park that parallels the length of the main street, a

The first mixed-use development constructed within the traditional neighborhood district, Birkdale is a 52-acre pedestrian-oriented project near major transportation routes.

Main Street, the major commercial hub of Birkdale, has modest on-street parking with larger parking structures hidden behind mixed-use buildings.

village green at the center of the development, and 10-foot-wide (3.05-meter-wide) sidewalks along Main Street. The grid street pattern links Birkdale Village to the surrounding neighborhood, which includes 491 single-family homes and townhouses on 137 acres (55.44 hectares) to the north. The residences, part of the new urbanist Greens at Birkdale Village, were developed at the same time as the mixed-use village center.

Management of the residential units has posed some challenges in setting rents and showing available floor plans. The high level of demand for upper-level, main-street residential units was underestimated. Even with rents priced at 15 to 30 percent above the area average, demand still outstripped supply. As units have turned over, rents have increased to be more in equilibrium with demand. The most popular units command a 30 to 50 percent premium compared with similar apartments in the area. In early 2007, Birkdale Village apartment rents were $660 to $1,110 per month for one-bedroom units, $1,110 to $1,900 for a two-bedroom apartment, and $1,420 to $2,220 per month for three-bedroom models. The wide variety in floor plans—45 different possibilities in 320 units—made showing units to prospective renters somewhat more challenging, especially in the initial lease-up. Management narrowed the possibilities by budget and location to identify the most appropriate units for potential tenants. Apartment occupancy rates in 2006 were typically about 96 percent, slightly higher than average for comparable multifamily properties in the area.

**Birkdale's design reflects Huntersville's commitment to public spaces and pedestrian connectivity.**

COURTESY OF PATRICK SCHNEIDER

# Downtown Redevelopement, Evanston, Illinois

Evanston, Illinois, is a first-ring suburb located directly north of and sharing a border with the city of Chicago. Since the 1950s, and in the face of competition from suburban shopping centers and office parks, downtown Evanston has evolved into a more diverse urban center, with substantial recent residential, retail, and entertainment development.

The city used a variety of means to encourage downtown redevelopment. Among these are plans, zoning changes, a special service district, and two tax increment financing (TIF) districts. In addition, the city added a Planned Development Ordinance to the zoning code, a mechanism by which the city council and developers negotiate development agreements. This ordinance helped lead to the residential and retail building boom that began in the late 1990s, which not only increased density in the downtown but also enhanced street-level retail and improved the pedestrian environment.

*For more information:*

City of Evanston Downtown Planning Project
http://www.cityofevanston.org/departments/
    communitydevelopment/planning/
    downtown-plan.shtml

*Contact information:*

Dennis Marino
Planning Division Director/Assistant
    Director of Community Development
City of Evanston
847-866-2928
dmarino@cityofevanston.org

Situated north of Chicago, the city of Evanston has used a mix of policies to encourage compact, mixed-use development along existing transit routes.

COURTESY OF ELS

## Evanston Overview

Evanston's population is growing slowly, yet this growth is largely encouraged by downtown residential development. Evanston has approximately 38,000 jobs. Major employers include Northwestern University, two hospitals located in the city, the school district, and the headquarters of Rotary International.

Founded and settled in the 1800s, Evanston has housing stock that dates to the early 1900s. The city is primarily located on a street grid system that includes a network of sidewalks and alleys. By the 1940s, the city was mostly built out, and its population peaked at 80,000 in 1970 before beginning a slow decline to 73,000 by 1990. Since 1990, infill housing development, mostly in the downtown, has resulted in a population increase to about 77,000 as of 2007.

Downtown Evanston encompasses a 30-square-block area in the center of the city. Northwestern University, with a total enrollment of about 13,000 full-time students, borders downtown to the north and east. Lake Michigan is located approximately one-half mile (0.8 km) to the east of the downtown core. With the exception of the Northwestern campus, stable residential neighborhoods border the downtown on all sides, thus preventing it from expanding its boundaries by development in any surrounding area. Instead, redevelopment must occur within the downtown boundaries, mostly at greater density.

Evanston has several assets that benefit its downtown and the city at large. As the first suburb north of the Chicago city limits, it has good access to the city and downtown Chicago, known as "the Loop." Evanston is served by the Chicago Transit Authority's (CTA) Purple Line and Metra commuter rail service, as well as CTA and PACE bus service, providing excellent access to both downtown Chicago and the greater metropolitan area. Lake Michigan is a key recreational amenity. Northwestern University is a major incubator for talent and a generator of downtown retail and housing demand.

## Government and Political Structure

Evanston operates using a council management form of government. Elected officials include a mayor and nine aldermen. The city manager reports to them and is the chief executive officer of all government divisions of the city.

Proposed developments, particularly those greater than 25 units or 20,000 square feet (1,858 square meters) that use the Planned Development Ordinance, go through the planning commission. The planning commission serves at the pleasure of the mayor, who also appoints an economic development committee for decisions specifically pertaining to tax increment financing.

For decades, the city council has been proactive about increasing the city's tax base through development and redevelopment. It has also recognized how larger development trends can affect real estate development in Evanston.

## Policies and Programs

Downtown Evanston is a historic urban center dating to the 19th century and is one of the few downtowns in the northern Chicago suburbs. Like many downtowns, it was a center of employment and retail, including department stores such as Marshall Field's and Sears. Retail competition, in the form of automobile-oriented shopping centers, began to have a negative effect on the retail stores in downtown Evanston as early as the 1960s. By 1980, most department stores, grocers, and other significant retailers had left the downtown.

Since the 1960s, downtown Evanston has tried to revitalize itself in the face of a declining retail base. The city has historically been adept at recognizing market trends and opportunities. In the 1970s, it sought to attract office development, followed by the creation of a research park in the 1980s. Both efforts were aimed at revitalizing the downtown, and both are viewed as successes, although each ran its course because of various market forces, and the city sought a new direction in the 1990s.

The city's overarching goals are to create a strong and vibrant mixed-use downtown, with residential, retail, entertainment, and institutional uses. The city sought to add residential units to the downtown, replace office jobs that had been lost, and reposition the downtown retail market, including making downtown more of an entertainment destination. Successful implementation of these goals also increases the city's tax base.

A key part of achieving greater density is the Planned Development Ordinance. Historically, the zoning districts for downtown Evanston allowed a building height no greater than 85 feet (25.91 meters). Beginning in the 1960s, exceptions to the building height limits were possible through a "planned development" process that allowed

greater heights on certain projects. Over the next couple of decades, the city and developers negotiated a number of planned developments, much as a planned unit development is negotiated.

The new 1993 zoning ordinance updated and formalized the Planned Development Ordinance. Developers proposing a downtown project could use the planned development process to seek additional height and density in return for a range of amenities or design criteria. Planned developments allow substantial additional height, in some cases up to 220 feet (67.06 meters) or more, depending on what the city and the developer negotiate. This ordinance has resulted in the construction of several high-rise residential towers since 1993.

Conditions for developers under the Planned Development Ordinance include ensuring that the project be compatible with surrounding developments in terms of height, bulk, and scale. Each project must enhance the character of downtown, provide streetscape amenities, and include street-level retail space.

Planned developments in Evanston require developers to "speak to" open space as part of the project. This requirement does not bind the devel-

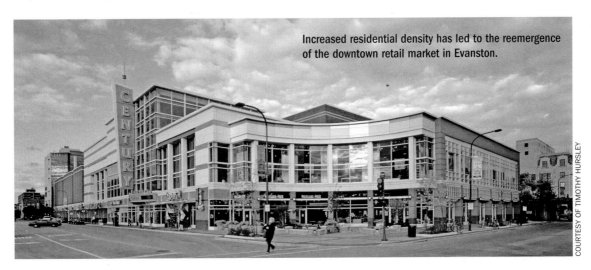

**Increased residential density has led to the reemergence of the downtown retail market in Evanston.**

COURTESY OF TIMOTHY HURSLEY

oper to provide open space as part of development, but it allows the city to negotiate with developers to do so as part of the overall approval process. As a result, developments typically include a number of public benefits, such as a small plaza or open space and, most typically, enhanced streetscaping.

A significant condition of the Planned Development Ordinance is for the proposed development to strengthen the pedestrian realm of the area. This condition includes appropriate pedestrian connections to surrounding development, adequate sidewalk widths, and attractive streetscaping.

Several amendments have been made to the Planned Development Ordinance. Most significantly, a 2004 amendment requires that any project with 25 or more units or greater than 20,000 square feet (1,858 square meters) must go through the planned development process, which encompasses nearly all proposed projects. Whereas before

PHOTO BY SAM NEWBERG

**In exchange for height and density bonuses, Evanston's Planned Development Ordinance requires the inclusion of streetscape amenities and ground-floor retail with new development.**

2004, developers could choose to use the Planned Development Ordinance, it is now required.

The pedestrian environment and streetscape is an ongoing issue. Starting in the 1960s, some towers were developed in the downtown that were allowed additional height but were surrounded by plazas and open space, lacking retail storefronts and not adding to the pedestrian realm. Changes in the 1993 ordinance required new development of any height to have retail or other building frontage constructed at the sidewalk edge. Combined with streetscaping, this retail use helped enhance the pedestrian environment. A formal set of design guidelines was passed in 2006 that is intended to improve the streetscape downtown.

A 2007 amendment to the Planned Development Ordinance addresses affordable housing. Developers must either set aside 10 percent of their units as affordable or pay a fee in lieu of affordable units. The fee is used for the creation of affordable units elsewhere throughout the city.

## Other Factors

The Planned Development Ordinance is the primary legal tool that allows greater density in Evanston. However, a number of other factors contribute to the developments that actually are built, including downtown and comprehensive plans, two TIF districts, a special services district, infrastructure enhancements, and real estate market conditions and trends.

A 1989 Downtown Plan sought increased economic development and a range of activities, all at a human scale. The updated comprehensive plan in 2000 further refined development goals, with a greater focus on aesthetics and amenities. As of early 2008, the 1989 Downtown Plan is being updated; a draft is plan available on the city's Web site for public review.

PHOTO BY SAM NEWBERG

Evanston's Planned Development Ordinance encourages developers to consider the public realm in the design process by providing pedestrian links to neighboring developments.

Tax increment financing provided assistance for initial projects in the mid-1990s and, more recently, for public parking ramps as part of two major downtown redevelopment projects. Without TIF, several key projects would have been much more difficult, if not impossible, to develop. TIF was also used to create the research park in the 1980s.

The city and developers have taken advantage of a changing retail market. Evanston was a dry city until the 1970s, and since prohibition was lifted, it has become a much more established destination for restaurants, bars, and live music. Retail has evolved, too. Department stores have not been replaced, but the downtown now has a movie theater, a public library built in 1989 (an attraction, though not retail), an established grocery store (Whole Foods), three bookstores, and several clothiers, providing both convenience and destination retail options. The movie theater is perhaps the biggest attraction, but the overall mix, including the Whole Foods, library, and restaurants, has in turn encouraged the residential development market.

Transit is a key component to the success of downtown Evanston. The city in 1993 partnered with the CTA to rebuild and enhance the Davis Street station and viaduct. The renovated CTA station at Davis Street accommodates CTA trains and buses, as well as PACE suburban buses. The Metra station is adjacent to the CTA station, providing a fourth form of mass transit to the downtown.

Evanston has encouraged transit-oriented development around each of its five CTA stations. Development around the Davis Street station, which, with Metra and bus connections, is the busiest Evanston station, has been the most prolific. Transit usage has also increased as development has occurred, which reduces the need for parking downtown.

With the approval of nearly all downtown Evanston business owners, the city council created a special services district in 1989: EVMARK, which stands for Evanston Marketing. Properties in the district are taxed to raise funding for maintenance, physical improvements, and marketing. No less than 50 percent of funds can be used for marketing, and up to 50 percent can be used for physical improvements. EVMARK handles sidewalk cleaning and snow removal, holiday lighting, business recruitment, and local advertising and assists the city with streetscape construction and repair.

EVMARK has a sunset clause and must be renewed periodically by the city council. It has had a significant effect on the downtown, helping create demand for space that has resulted in greater densities in recent projects, and the city council will likely renew EVMARK on an ongoing basis.

## Results and Reaction

A significant amount of new development has occurred in downtown Evanston since the mid-1990s, which has made it much more healthy and dynamic. This development has occurred as a result of changing demographics, a strong residential market, and various city policies—most notably the 1993 zoning update that included the current version of the Planned Development Ordinance. Since 1996, nearly 2,500 housing units have been built, have been approved, or are under construction in downtown Evanston. The vast majority are owner-occupied condominiums.

Completed in 1997, one of the first major developments was the Park Evanston, a 24-story, 265-unit apartment project with 40,000 square feet (3,716 square meters) of retail anchored by a Whole Foods store. Because Park Evanston was one of the first major residential mixed-use developments in Evanston, it relied heavily on TIF to "prime the pump" and help finance the project in a still unproven high-rise apartment market in the area.

Another significant mixed-use project is a retail, movie theater, hotel, and high-rise residential tower that opened in three phases between 2000 and 2003. It includes an 18-screen Century Theater; a 175-room Hilton Garden Inn; a significant office component; retail development, including a Borders bookstore and Urban Outfitters; and a 207-unit, 28-story Optima Views condominium tower.

Another major project is Sherman Plaza, which opened in 2006. It contains 252 condominiums, a large fitness center, and more than 150,000 square feet (13,935 square meters) of retail space anchored by Barnes & Noble. Sherman Plaza is featured at the end of this case study.

**Multimodal transit provides residents of Evanston with a variety of transportation options.**

PHOTO BY SAM NEWBERG

The city council used TIF for the preceding two projects, albeit in a more limited way, to build a parking structure to accompany each. The two ramps total over 3,000 spaces and serve not only the respective projects but also the parking needs of the greater area around each.

The use of TIF has had dramatic results. For example, in 1985, when the Research Park TIF district was created, the existing properties in that area were assessed at $1.8 million by the city. The TIF district includes development of the research park as well as the Hilton, theater, Optima tower, and retail uses. As of 2005, the assessed value had jumped to $104 million. The assessed value would be substantially less if increased density were not allowed using the Planned Development Ordinance.

A major factor accounting for the development that has occurred in Evanston is its location within the greater Chicago area. Its proximity and access to Chicago, high-quality transit service, location along Lake Michigan, and reputation as an educated city because of the presence of Northwestern all are significant amenities.

Demographics also factor into the success of Evanston, particularly residential development in the downtown. Baby boomers are increasingly empty nesters, and many are choosing a downtown lifestyle in a condominium. The children of baby boomers, known as echo boomers, are finishing school and forming households, but many are not yet forming families or do not choose a single-family home, and condominiums are another option for ownership. Downtown Evanston offers housing choices for both categories. Evanston has not historically been a strong residential choice for the cohort age 25 to 34 years, but that is changing because of its increasingly vibrant downtown.

## Lessons Learned

The city's use of various policies to increase the tax base and maintain a vibrant downtown has been successful in Evanston. The city recognized the market potential for various uses and has most recently taken advantage of strong demand for residential and new forms of retail development.

The Planned Development Ordinance, in particular, has provided the city with a way not only to allow greater densities but also to improve its livability. As continued development occurs, the city makes changes and adjustments in the ordinance, such as an affordable-housing requirement and design standards.

Not everyone is happy with the amount of development that has occurred or the height of some towers. The public has some concern that development is happening too fast. The city council and planning department are revisiting this issue, and they have addressed it in an updated Downtown Plan that, as of early 2008, is undergoing public review. The city is also considering a hybrid form-based zoning code for particular downtown street sections with a historic character the city would like to see preserved.

Sidewalk widths have been an issue with some recent downtown development. The sidewalks in front of the Borders, Hilton Garden Inn, and Century Theater project are now considered too narrow and require expansion. Sidewalk widths in subsequent developments, particularly the Sherman Plaza project, are substantially wider and deemed more adequate for the downtown.

## Featured Development: Sherman Plaza

Sherman Plaza is the most recent large-scale, mixed-use project to be developed in downtown Evanston. Located on one of the core blocks of the downtown, it contains a variety of uses, including a 26-story residential tower and a city-financed parking garage. Sherman Plaza replaced a vacant Osco drugstore and an aging, decrepit, city-owned parking garage.

Located on the block bounded by Sherman Avenue, Church Street, Benson Avenue, and Davis Street, the intersection of Sherman and Church is considered the 100 percent corner of downtown. As a result, the main anchor retail tenant, Barnes & Noble, occupies the corner space. Additional retailers are located around the block at street level, including an LA Fitness Club.

The residential component consists of 252 condominium units priced from $260,000 to $1.7 million. First move-ins occurred in 2006, and the condominiums were nearly sold out as of May 2007.

Two key elements that allowed Sherman Plaza to move forward were the city's use of TIF to construct a parking garage for the project and the density and height allowed using the planned development process. This process ensured several aspects of the project design met with the city's principles for downtown.

The sidewalks, particularly along Sherman Avenue, are wide, with extensive streetscaping. Retail storefronts exist on all four sides of the block, even at the base of the parking garage. The residential tower is set back from Church Street to reduce shadows on neighboring uses to the north.

The mixed-use Sherman Plaza anchors a key corner of downtown Evanston.

PHOTO BY SAM NEWBERG

# Plantation Midtown District, Plantation, Florida

The plan for the Plantation Midtown District seeks to transform a suburban, predominantly commercial district into a more-urban town center where residents can live, work, and play. To guide this effort, the city developed and adopted a conceptual master plan and a new zoning code. The process of developing and adopting the changes took roughly two years, beginning in 2002 and adopting the final regulations in 2004. Strategies to achieve the desired outcome include economic development, diversification of land uses to include more residential and recreational uses, classification of streets and regulation of the bulk and massing of buildings to foster compatibility with pedestrian-friendly street life, and conversion of the car-oriented district to a multimodal environment with increased walkability and transit use.

*Contact information:*

Laurence Leeds, AICP

Planning, Zoning and Economic
    Development Director

City of Plantation

Department of Planning, Zoning, and
    Economic Development

401 NW 70 Terrace

Plantation, FL 33317

lleeds@plantation.org

954-797-2622

*Web site:*

Plantation Midtown

http://www.plantation.org/pzed/midtown/
    index.html

## Community Information

Located ten miles (16.1 km) west of Fort Lauderdale in the heart of Broward County, Plantation was established in 1953 as a bedroom community. Home to 85,000 residents in 2006, Plantation contains a mix of retail, office, hotel, and residential land uses common to suburban South Florida. Major employers include several large national firms, including American Express, Motorola, Broadspire Services (formerly Kemper Services), and DHL. Residential development is largely single-family homes with some low-rise multifamily units. The city is accessible from the east by the Florida Turnpike and Interstate 95, from the south by Interstate 595, and from the west by the Sawgrass Expressway.

The Plantation Midtown District is in the center of the city and covers 860 acres (348 hectares) with boundaries of University Drive to the east, Interstate 595 to the south, Pine Island Road to the west, and Cleary Boulevard to the north. It is the largest commercial district in the city with approximately 3 million square feet (278,709 square meters) of office space (two-thirds Class A) and 2.5 million square feet (232,258 square meters) of retail space that houses regional shopping centers, government and community services, and national and regional corporate headquarters. Businesses in the district employ approximately 45,000 people.

## Local Government Structure

Plantation is run by a strong mayor and city council with five at-large members. Areas of focus include business district redevelopment, neighborhood improvement, and efficient government operations and procedures.

Plans for the Plantation Midtown District are guided by the Midtown Advisory Board, which includes seven members who must be businesspersons or property owners within the district. Terms of appointment are one year. The mayor and each member of the city council appoint one board member, and the seventh appointee is named on a rotating basis by a different city council member. The Midtown Advisory Board meets monthly, and the city planning department consults with members regularly about redevelopment plans for the district.

In addition, the Plantation Planning and Zoning Board reviews all site plans and code changes for the Plantation Midtown District. The city council has final approval authority.

## Redevelopment of the Plantation Midtown District

In 2002, the city of Plantation hired a team of private local consulting firms—Keith and Schnars, P.A., Civic Design Associates, Lambert Advisory, and the Goodman Corporation—to prepare a conceptual master plan for the Plantation Midtown District, which included a community visioning process, a public charrette, a market analysis, and a mobility study. The initiative for a master plan grew out of earlier efforts that included a 2001 business revitalization plan for the area. The consulting team developed a nine-month visioning and planning process and gathered input from businesses in the area and community leaders. Major concerns identified in the process included traffic congestion, limitations in pedestrian accessibility, underperforming retail properties, and a desire for cultural and entertainment venues.

In addition, participants were asked for their preferences about the physical environment and given a variety of visual images to consider. The highest-ranking images indicated a clear preference for a pedestrian-friendly environment. The final product was the 2002 Central Plantation Conceptual Master Plan to revitalize the area that would later be renamed the Plantation Midtown District.

The real estate market analysis conducted as part of the planning effort indicated that although no new demand for retail existed, improving the design and layout of the retail space at existing malls would significantly enhance their appeal for tenants and customers. The analysis of the residential market calculated a near-term demand (2003 to 2007) for an additional 950 housing units in the Plantation Midtown area.

The plan seeks to find opportunities to reduce the need for cars in and around the district. All the major streets at the boundaries of the Plantation Midtown District are currently at capacity, so new development faces challenges from a concurrency standpoint. Because many of the concerns about the future of the area were transportation related, the city

was able to partner with the Florida Department of Transportation in the preparation of the conceptual plan. The department provided $200,000 in matching funds toward the planning process, specifically for transportation and traffic initiatives.

Other funding included $4.5 million in Broward County redevelopment grants and allocations from the state legislature. In 2003, the city underwrote the launching of designated capital projects relating to the district through a $3 million bond.

The final conceptual master plan outlined a recommended redevelopment plan, a master plan for managing growth, a plan for multimodal mobility, a capital improvement plan, and an implementation schedule for a 25-year timeline. The redevelopment plan calls for increasing the square footage of each land use within the Plantation Midtown District in phases, based on the availability of undeveloped land, existing building conditions, and conclusions from a market analysis and mobility study. Plan implementation uses a variety of techniques, including regulatory incentives, design guidelines, revenue enhancements, public improvements, and working with the private sector to maximize public and private investments.

In 2004, the city created a new zoning district, the SPI-3 (Special Public Interest district, one of three in the city) or the Plantation Midtown Code, to implement development standards based on the recommendations of the conceptual master plan. The zoning district has guided the conversion of the district from a predominantly suburban development pattern to a denser and more active mixed-use town center. The code is designed to foster the appropriate integration and performance of land uses within a mixed-use context rather than simply regulate land uses. Many of the results are encouraged through an incentive structure that grants additional development rights in exchange for the appropriate development characteristics.

**Density.** The new zoning code seeks to promote the development of tightly integrated mixed-use buildings and sites. The city's land use plan permits residential density of up to 25 dwelling units per acre based on gross acreage of the overall site. However, under the SPI-3 zoning, if a developer builds residential infill without overall site redevelopment, density is instead determined based on the "equivalent site area" in an effort to base density calculation exclusively on the residential area of the mixed-use site. The code defines equivalent site area as only the acreage associated with the footprint of the residential infill structure.

The original policy allowed developers in the Plantation Midtown District to build higher densities of up to 30 to 50 dwelling units per acre

COURTESY OF ADD, INC./VATHAUER STUDIOS

The Plantation Midtown Conceptual Plan is designed to transform a largely suburban area into a vibrant, mixed-use district.

of equivalent site area in exchange for a per unit impact fee (designed to compensate for anticipated increased demands on infrastructure) for each unit over the citywide maximum of 25 units per acre. City planners report that, in practice, a per unit fee was never adopted; instead, developers proposed in lieu of the fee to build the needed infrastructure to support the density increase. In 2007, a code revision is underway to require the developer to construct any needed infrastructure to support the development proposal rather than offer the option of a fee.

**Urban Design: Streets.** The Plantation Midtown District master plan seeks to develop a more orderly internal street network within the neighborhood. The accompanying land use regulations establish a street classification system and incentives designed to promote more-compact, pedestrian-friendly development.

The location of different types of development is based on the classification of the fronting street rather than the block.

**Urban Design: Buildings.** The Plantation Midtown District code carefully guides the bulk and massing of buildings in an effort to achieve a pedestrian-friendly, human-scaled environment, instituting requirements for building placement and frontage, as well as setbacks and build-to zones.

In addition, the code indicates required building step-backs as guided by street classifications. For example, on B streets, building floors above three stories must have a step-back of at least 20 feet (6.10 meters) from the street facade, whereas on A streets the same requirement applies for floors above five stories.

**Connectivity.** Increasing multimodal access is a major emphasis of the conceptual plan. To ensure that new development is pedestrian-friendly, the SPI-3 zone encourages development with relatively small setbacks on designated pedestrian streets. The capital plan also calls for developing a trolley system for the area and increasing the availability of sidewalks.

The Midtown Conceptual Plan regulates streetscape improvements based on a hierarchical street classification system.

The Plantation Midtown Trolley launched in February 2007, providing free transportation to designated stops on two loops throughout the district every ten minutes, five days a week from 7 a.m. to 7 p.m. The service area will gradually be expanded in a three-phase rollout of the system.

**Open Space and Parks.** Higher-density development can create the need for open space to mitigate the impact of the more-intensive development. For this reason, the creation of an open-space network for pedestrian enjoyment is a key component of the Midtown plan. Envisioned amenities include mall and park plazas, an amphitheater, a jogging trail, landscaping, a lakeside promenade, an esplanade, street trees, pedestrian-oriented lighting, benches, trash receptacles, and irrigation. The capital plan also calls for developing a transit greenway that connects to two other greenways in Broward County.

**Parking.** The conceptual master plan seeks to reduce the number of parking spaces needed and find ways to manage the demand for parking in the district more efficiently. In addition, the code calls for placing parking behind buildings and provides various methods for reducing the required quantities of on-site parking. Reduced parking ratios are available in exchange for certain incentives, such as cross access to adjacent parking lots and shared parking. Before 2007, developers could also pay a fee of $6,500 per space to reduce the number of required spaces. The fees went into a Midtown parking fund designated to finance the city's construction of structured parking within the district.

## PLANTATION MIDTOWN DISTRICT

## Street Classifications and Design Standards

**A Streets:** A streets are characterized by minimal setbacks, active commercial frontage at the ground floor, taller and more intensive buildings fronting the street, and a consistent streetwall. A streets typically feature a number of traffic-calming measures as well as a full complement of pedestrian amenities, including wide sidewalks, on-street parking, and well-developed streetscape. A streets are the principal "town center" streets and are intended to be used by pedestrians and slow-moving traffic as the primary transit routes.

**B Streets:** B streets are similar to A streets, although less intensively developed; they are still urban in terms of pedestrian traffic, characterized by a small setback and a relatively consistent streetwall. B streets are more residential in nature but might also have smaller-scale commercial uses.

**C Streets:** C streets are the large, regional arterials bounding the district, as well as Broward Boulevard and Peters Road. They are intended primarily for efficient vehicular movement. They are characterized by large setbacks with landscape buffers, although they should also be able to accommodate access points with enhanced signage and gateway elements.

**D Streets:** D Streets are more suburban in nature, characterized by larger setbacks and less building frontage. D Streets are located in quieter areas but are also used as the "back streets" for the town-center areas, where elements such as surface parking and loading docks are located.

In addition, streets in the district are subject to specific design standards, including the following:

- Sidewalks at all lot frontages;
- Curbside parking provided wherever possible on A and B streets; and
- Landscaping in the right-of-way between the curb and the sidewalk.

*Source: SPI-3 Plantation Midtown Code.*

## Plan Implementation

Developer interest in the redevelopment of the Plantation Midtown District has been strong. For example, while the original plan recommended the addition of 950 housing units in the first phase of implementation, the private sector has proposed nearly 2,000 rental and for-sale units in various projects.

Planning staff meets regularly with developers to work out details and ensure a clear understanding of code compliance. The new zoning code is quite specific about design and massing of new developments, such as building setbacks and height, and directs new and redevelopment projects toward upper-end construction and building materials. The regulations also have requirements regarding creating high-quality open space and landscaping amenities.

Public response to the redevelopment of the Plantation Midtown District has been limited, in part because little residential development exists that would yield an immediate constituency. Some businesses have watched new project proposals carefully and voiced concerns about increased density, particularly with regard to its impact on traffic congestion. One older, two-story residential community nearby has been vocal in its concerns about the proposed height of some redevelopment proposals that could include buildings of ten and 18 stories.

One significant administrative change that has been adopted for the SPI-3 zone is to allow the city council to approve waivers to development regulations. The original proposal did not allow such waivers. Planning staff presents such requests to the city council, indicating whether it supports a waiver application. In reviewing a waiver request, city council members consider the overall quality of the project and its consistency with the vision for the district, as well as what obstacles prevent full compliance.

## New Development for the Plantation Midtown District

Several new projects are under construction or proposed for development for the reconfigured mixed-use plan for the Plantation Midtown District. Interest in adding a residential component to create mixed-use properties has been particularly strong.

Following are some of the new and proposed developments:

■ **Veranda at Plantation:** The first development under construction features 380 condominiums and 16 three-story townhouses on 25 acres (10.12 hectares). It also includes a 45,000-square-foot (4,181-square-meter) shopping center and a 28,000-square-foot (2,601-square-meter) Publix supermarket.

■ **The Residences at the Fountains:** A residential addition to the Fountains Mall retail site that will include 478 residential units, including 36 live/work units, is proposed. (See "Featured Development" for more detail.)

■ **One Plantation Place:** A 15-acre (6.07-hectare) mixed-use redevelopment of the existing University Shops shopping center, plans call for 30,000 square feet (2,787 square meters) of commercial office space, 80,000 square feet (7,432 square meters) of retail space, and two towers with 574 condominium and townhouse residences. The project would relocate existing tenants such as McDonald's, Goodyear Tire, Kinko's, and IHOP into new facilities within the development.

■ **321 North:** This 33-acre (13.35-hectare) project includes redevelopment of the largely vacant 650,000-square-foot (60,387-square-meter) enclosed Fashion Mall, a 114,000-square-foot (10,591-square-meter) office pavilion, and a

Sheraton Suites Hotel. The project will require demolition and reconstruction of significant portions of the enclosed mall to create new, outward-facing retail space. When it is completed, 321 North will contain approximately 550,000 square feet (51,097 square meters) of retail space, 300,000 to 400,000 square feet (27,887 to 37,161 square meters) of class A office space, and 400 to 600 residential units.

■ **The Regency:** This three-acre (1.21-hectare) property is currently developed with four one-story office and commercial buildings. The applicant proposes to demolish the existing buildings and construct a nine-story mixed-use building. The building will face NW 82nd Avenue with retail, restaurant, and office uses on the ground floor; additional office use on floors two through six; and residential use on floors seven through nine. The building wraps a six-level parking garage that will accommodate the commercial as well as the residential uses. Nearby properties include the Fashion Mall to the north, retail to the east (Toys "R" Us and Petco), an office/bank building to the south, and NW 82nd Avenue to the west.

## Lessons Learned

Transforming the suburban single-use character of the Plantation Midtown District into a vibrant mixed-use community has been an ongoing process, requiring visionary planning, the coordination of all parties involved, and the facilitation of communication between actors and stakeholders. The development team found the following actions essential in creating the plan:

**Establish a sustainable foundation of support for the plan.** The plan for the Plantation Midtown District seeks to reshape the character of the area significantly and has a total buildout of 25 years. Therefore, ensuring solid political and administra-

tive support is critical to follow-through on long-term implementation.

**Learn the ropes of compact development.** The Plantation planning and zoning staff was well versed in suburban development. However, the switch to more-urban, compact development being promoted in the Plantation Midtown District is a new endeavor with its own learning curve. Professional development opportunities helped the staff learn more about urban design and development. Developers have also found helpful engaging architects with demonstrated experience in compact development to design appropriate projects that are likely to require less review and modification for approval.

**Visit other communities to see on-the-ground examples.** To determine the preferable architectural styles and layout for the transformation of the Plantation Midtown District to a mixed-use town center, planning staff visited nearby communities with similar patterns of development.

**Create a design book.** Planning staff compiled examples of desired styles and amenities and assembled them in a "tool book" for the development community to consult for visual models of preferred practices.

**Meet with the developer early and often.** Planning staff has found that frequent communication with the development team, particularly early in the process, has been important to guide projects toward a desirable outcome that is compliant with the SPI-3 zoning code. For most effectiveness, a cross section of the development team—including landscaping and engineering—should be involved in meeting with city planners.

**Depend more on regulations than guidelines to implement the plan.** Although the conceptual plan for the Plantation Midtown District was very clear in its vision, the SPI-3 code relies heavily on suggested guidelines for implementation. A code that calls for mandatory, rather than voluntary, compliance would provide more certainty in realizing the vision for Midtown.

**Coordinate the plan with other city departments.** Including other city departments, such as engineering and utilities, early in the process—while a consultant was producing the land development regulations—would have prevented the need for some later code revisions.

**Consider mixed-use buildings.** Thus far, many proposals have been for mixed-use sites but not necessarily mixed-use buildings. Regulations could have included bonuses or incentives to encourage the development of office, retail, or residential in the same building, which would further reduce the demand for automobile-based travel.

Designed to incorporate an existing open-air shopping center, the Fountains consists of two residential towers, ground-floor retail, and a pedestrian plaza.

COURTESY OF ADD, INC.

## Featured Development: The Fountains

The Fountains Mall is a 415,000-square-foot (38,555-square-meter) open-air shopping center on the west side of University Drive between Interstate 595 and Broward Boulevard. The 60-acre (24.28-hectare) site will soon include 478 residential units built on existing surface parking lots on eight acres (3.24 hectares) at the rear of the shopping center site. Known as the Residences at the Fountains, the property will consist of two luxury residential apartment towers of 11 and 12 stories. The building will include studio and one-, two-, and three-bedroom rental units, ranging in size from approximately 639 to 1,970 square feet (59 to 183 square meters). Each building will have a central two-story atrium lobby, a cyber café, and fitness and business center on the ground floor. The fourth floor of each tower will offer recreational amenities, including a lap pool, spa, and fountains. Thirty-six live/work units are part of the project.

By right, this 8.74-acre (3.54-hectare) infill project was subject to the "equivalent site area" density formula of the SPI-3 zoning, which, in its strictest interpretation, would have allowed up to 218 dwelling units. Instead, the developer applied for and received a waiver from the city council for increased density based on an allocation of 478 allowable residential units from a pool known as "flexibility units"[1] for the Residences at the Fountains.

The site will provide parking for 943 cars, including 142 curbside spaces and 71 open spaces. The remaining 730

spaces will be built in three levels of garage parking divided between each apartment community. To enhance a pedestrian-friendly street front, the three-story live/work units will wrap around the ground floor of each of the garages. The property will also have a transit stop and a one-acre (0.4-hectare) linear park with bike storage.

The Residences at the Fountains contains several of the recommended design features for the Plantation Midtown District, such as buildings located at the designated build-to line, step-backs of

Aerial map of proposed site of the Fountains.

building facades, reduction of the scale of the large site with an interior grid street, improvements to the east-west corridor for vehicular and pedestrian accessibility, and creation of a pedestrian plaza. Several landscaped pedestrian paths and street connections will link the existing Fountains shopping center to the Residences at the Fountains to realize the vision of the Plantation Midtown District as a mixed-use, urban village. Each intersection within the property will also feature enhanced landscaping.

Groundbreaking for Phase I of the Residences at the Fountains is expected to start in early 2008, with the construction of 239 of the dwelling units.

The existing shopping plaza, which was constructed in the 1980s, was recently sold to Developers Diversified Realty. Renovations to the retail property have commenced, and the new shops are expected to open by 2009.

COURTESY OF ADD, INC./VATHAUER STUDIOS

**Planned pedestrian pathways link the residential and retail components of the Fountains to create a mixed-use urban village.**

**The project's ground-floor retail is designed with 36 live/work units, a fitness and business center, and a cyber café.**

COURTESY OF ADD, INC.

1. Flexibility units are residential units designated in 125 geographic areas throughout the county called flexibility zones and identified in the Broward County Future Land Use Map. These are discretionary units that a local government can assign, pending project approval, to allow flexibility in density patterns. The number of allowable flex units in a flexibility zone is determined by the difference between the number of dwelling units permitted within the zone under the Broward County Comprehensive Plan and the smaller number of dwelling units permitted within the same area by the local government, such as under the Plantation Comprehensive Plan.

# New Model Colony, Ontario, California

In January 1998, the city of Ontario adopted the New Model Colony General Plan to serve as the guide for the development of an 8,200-acre (3,318.42-hectare) tract of land that had been part of an agricultural preserve. The city officially annexed the area in November 1999 and renamed it the "New Model Colony" (NMC).

The goal of the NMC General Plan is the creation of a diverse mixed-use community with a public realm that promotes pedestrian activity. Encompassing 13 square miles (33.67 square km), the NMC is planned to become a place of diverse uses, comprising a mix of residential neighborhoods; high-intensity regional-serving centers, employment nodes, and schools; and an activity core that serves as the common focal point for all neighborhoods and districts. In addition, each neighborhood will be connected to the others through a network of greenways, trails, and open space.

*Contact information:*

Scott Murphy, Principal Planner

E-mail: smurphy@ci.ontario.ca.us

Department of City Planning,
   New Model Colony

303 East "B" Street

Ontario, CA 91764

*Web site:*

http://www.ci.ontario.ca.us

## Community Information

The city of Ontario is located in San Bernardino County, approximately 35 miles (56.33 km) east of downtown Los Angeles. Incorporated in 1891, the city covers 50 square miles (129.5 square km). Ontario is a key center of the fast-growing Inland Empire region; its employment, population, retail sales, and industrial absorption have risen sharply over the past two decades. The city benefits from its proximity to major transportation arteries, including three major freeways and Ontario International Airport (OIA), which is the second-busiest airport in southern California in terms of passenger and air cargo. OIA is UPS's western regional distribution hub, making it an attractive location for firms moving packages.

For decades, southern California grew outward along its transportation corridors. As the region's urban core has been built out, both costs and congestion have encouraged outward migration of firms and people to the Inland Empire. As a result, the Inland Empire has captured a large share of the region's growth over the past 15 years.

Ontario has become the primary center of job growth in the Inland Empire in part because of its proximity to major transit nodes. Research by the California Employment Development Department suggests that, over the past 15 years, the employment base has more than doubled from 41,501 in 1991 to 82,000 in 2006. The key economic sectors in Ontario include distribution and transportation, manufacturing, and retail trade. A study commissioned by the city identified UPS (3,500 employees), Mag Instrument (1,000 employees), Verizon (679 employees), Burns International Security (650 employees), Marriott International Hotel (624 employees), and Toyota North America (530 employees) as being some of the city's major employers. In addition, the California Department of Finance's Demographic Research Unit found that the city's population has risen sharply over the past several decades from 133,000 in 1990 to 170,000 in 2006 (27 percent). According to the 2000 census, the majority of Ontario's housing units (57 percent) are owner occupied. The vast majority (60 percent) of the housing units in the city were built since 1970.

## About the New Model Colony

The New Model Colony is an 8,200-acre (3,318.42-hectare) area located in the southern-most portion of Ontario. The NMC includes approximately one-fourth of the city's area and is bounded by Riverside Drive to the north, Miliken Avenue and Hammer Avenue to the east, Riverside County line and Merril Avenue to the south, and Euclid Avenue on the west.

From the early 1900s through the 1990s, the NMC was dominated by dairy farms primarily operated by Portuguese, Dutch, and French Basque farmers. By the 1950s, southern California was the most productive dairy region in the United States, outproducing traditional dairy states such as Minnesota and Wisconsin.

In the 1990s, the escalating costs of operating southern California dairy farms and the demand for housing pressured farmers to consider relocating their dairies and annexing their land into adjacent cities. Reacting to these concerns, San Bernardino County dissolved its agricultural preserve and incorporated portions into three adjacent cities: Ontario, Chino, and Chino Hills. The city of Ontario annexed 8,200 acres (3,318.42 hectares) of the former agricultural preserve in 1999. As indicated in Table 1, when it began, the predominant land use within the New Model Colony was agricultural.

Surrounded on all sides by already built-out communities, the NMC is strategically positioned as one of the largest undeveloped tracts of land in the center of the Inland Empire. The NMC is currently in transition from a former farming area to a new, planned mixed-use community. The first new development in the NMC opened in spring 2007 at Edenglen, which comprises 160 acres (64.75 hectares) (see "Featured Development"). The remaining parcels in the NMC are in various stages of planning with buildout phased over the next 30 years.

## Community Government and Political Structure

The city of Ontario is governed by a five-member city council and a mayor who is directly elected by the voters. The city council and mayor appoint the Planning Commission. The Planning Department consists of four divisions: Administration, Current Planning, Advanced Planning, and the New Model

One of the largest tracts of undeveloped land in the Inland Empire, the 8,200-acre New Model Colony is being transformed from low-density agricultural uses into a collection of compact planned communities.

COURTESY OF CITY OF ONTARIO, PLANNING DEPARTMENT

## Table 1: NEW MODEL COLONY LAND USE DISTRIBUTION

| Land Use Category | Land Uses | Acres | Percentage of NMC |
|---|---|---|---|
| Agriculture | Dairy, Poultry, Other | 7,328.1 | 89.4 |
| Residential | Single-Family | 219.7 | |
| | Multifamily | 9.2 | |
| | **SUBTOTAL** | **228.9** | **2.8** |
| Commercial | Office | 0.7 | |
| | Retail | 18.3 | |
| | Other Commercial | 0.3 | |
| | **SUBTOTAL** | **19.3** | **0.2** |
| Industrial | Trucking, Manufacturing, Other | 67.3 | 0.8 |
| Institutional/Public | Roads, Utilities, Flood Control, Religious | 487.6 | 5.9 |
| Vacant | | 68.8 | 0.8 |
| **TOTAL** | | 8,200.0 | 100.0 |

*Source: City of Ontario, New Model Colony General Plan Amendment (1999).*

Colony. The Advanced Planning division conducted the planning and analysis that led to the creation of the NMC General Plan Amendment. However, as Ontario's planning director Jerry Blum notes, "We wanted a specialized team in place to implement the plans for the New Model Colony."

The NMC General Plan was actually an amendment to Ontario's existing General Plan, approved by the city council in January 1998. The plan designates the entire NMC area as a Specific Plan (SP) district. This SP zoning designation requires that the NMC be developed with a series of Specific Plans that carry out the objectives of the NMC General Plan. The city began accepting applications for Specific Plans in November 1999. To date, nine Specific Plan applications have been submitted to the city. The city approved the first Specific Plan in the NMC (called Edenglen) in November 2005. The city council must approve each Specific Plan. The Planning Commission is responsible for approving the tract maps and development plans that are particular to each of the Specific Plan areas.

## Policy Analysis

The New Model Colony is planned to encompass a mix of uses, including varied residential neighborhoods, retail, entertainment, offices, educational, medical, industrial, cultural, parks, and government. At completion of the anticipated 30-year buildout, the NMC is expected to be home to 100,000 residents in more than 30,000 housing units. With approximately 13 square miles (33.67 square km), the NMC would house 7,769 residents per square mile. By contrast, the rest of the city of Ontario currently has 4,594 residents per square mile.

The NMC General Plan calls for each neighborhood and center to be a distinctively identifiable

## City of Ontario New Model Colony General Plan Land Use Map

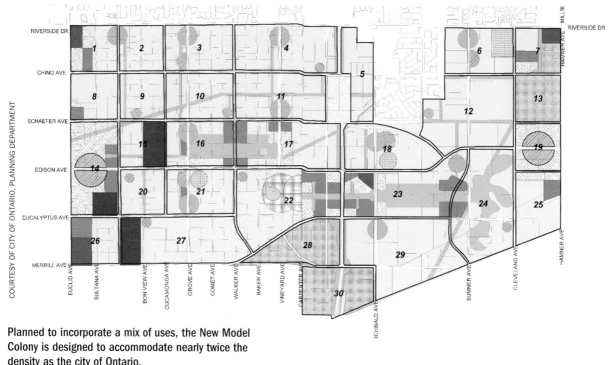

Planned to incorporate a mix of uses, the New Model Colony is designed to accommodate nearly twice the density as the city of Ontario.

The communities of the New Model Colony will be connected by a series of greenbelts and parkways.

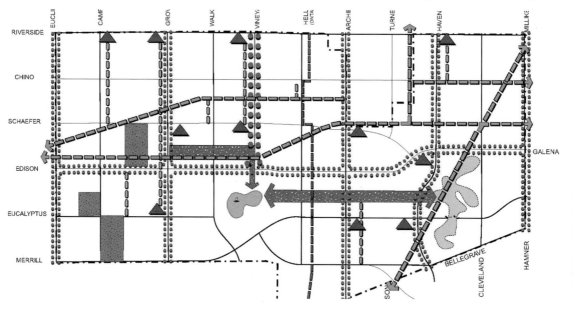

place for its residents, employees, and visitors. The neighborhoods of the NMC will be united through a network of greenways, open spaces, amenities, and infrastructure. The goal is to extend Ontario's fabric of development rather than isolate the NMC as an island. However, the NMC aims to distinguish itself by creating a mix of uses that emphasize pedestrian activity as a fundamental goal for all new development in the area. The new neighborhoods will be organized around a number of amenities, including a regional-scaled public park (or "Village Green") and extensively landscaped parkways and trails.

Although the primary land use planned is housing, the NMC plans also include 5.5 million square feet (510,967 square meters) of commercial space and 5.1 million square feet (473,806 square meters) of industrial space (Table 2). In addition, nearly one-quarter of the land will be dedicated to public uses, including 925 acres (374.33 hectares) of parks and trails, 20 elementary schools, five middle schools, three high schools, and an 80-acre (32.37-hectare) higher-learning campus.

The NMC will feature 11 distinct residential neighborhoods. They will be self-contained places that include a full panoply of uses. A diversity of housing types will be promoted in each neighborhood, ranging from small-lot detached or attached units to townhomes, apartments, and traditional single-family detached configurations.

The NMC General Plan calls for a town center to constitute the primary center of activity and identity for all the neighborhoods and districts of the NMC. Public spaces will be pedestrian oriented, and a series of public squares and parks will be developed to accommodate community events and gatherings.

Several high-intensity centers will accommodate uses that serve and attract a regional population

| Table 2: NMC LAND USE AT BUILDOUT | |
|---|---|
| Land Use | Percentage of NMC |
| Residential | |
| Single Family | 54 |
| Multifamily | 10 |
| Commercial | |
| Industrial | 6 |
| Public Amenities | 24 |

*Source: City of Ontario.*

and provide employment opportunities. Diverse "destination" uses may be accommodated, including regional and specialty retail, professional offices, medical and research facilities, and hotels and conference facilities. The Village Green will be developed as a major amenity of the NMC. The plans for the Village Green call for a concept similar to San Francisco's Golden Gate Park with similar passive recreational and cultural uses, including museums, outdoor performance venues, botanical gardens, and waterways.

## Process of Enacting the New Model Colony

By the early 1990s, aerial photos showed the area that would become the NMC to be a donut hole surrounded by urban land that was a prime target for urban development. In 1993, the San Bernardino County Board of Supervisors voted to consider dissolving the 14,000-acre (5,665.6-hectare) agricultural preserve's status. This action paved the way for the transition of the area from agricultural uses to a planned mixed-use community.

The Local Agency Formation Committee recommended the area's division among three neighboring cities—Ontario, Chino, and Chino Hills—with the largest share going to Ontario. With the decision to annex 8,200 acres (3,318.42 hectares) into

Ontario, the city began an extensive program of community involvement to create a consensus for how to develop the area. Table 3 summarizes the chronology of the enactment of the NMC General Plan and the annexation of the NMC into the city of Ontario.

In August 1995, the city council appointed the 16-member Agricultural Preserve Advisory Committee (APAC), which included the following stakeholder groups: Ontario residents, sphere of influence residents, business leaders, school district representatives, interest group spokespersons, and representatives of the Planning Commission. The APAC conducted 17 public meetings from 1995 through 1998, when the city council adopted the plan. The public was encouraged to speak at each APAC meeting. In addition, the city sponsored a series of public workshops in 1996 and 1997 to encourage the entire community's participation in the plan's formulation.

Although the annexation of 8,200 acres (3,318.42 hectares) of land represented an incredible opportunity for the city, the existing residents of Ontario were concerned about the costs associated with funding infrastructure needed to serve such a large area. To gain public support for both the NMC plan and the land annexation, the city council reassured existing Ontario residents that they would not foot the bill for the extensive infrastructure required.

The various stakeholder groups worked hard to create consensus and a common vision for the NMC. According to Ontario's planning director, for a successful plan, "Collaboration is key, and this includes collaboration among city planning staff, city staff, outside consultants, the development community and citizens." He notes further, "Honest, healthy working relationships with the development community are key." The common vision and goals the various stakeholders agreed to

## Table 3: CHRONOLOGY OF NMC GENERAL PLAN

| Date | Event |
|---|---|
| August 1995 | Agricultural Preserve Advisory Committee (APAC) appointed |
| November 1995 to April 1997 | Public meetings and workshops |
| April 1997 | APAC recommends approval to Planning Commission |
| May 1997 | Planning Commission begins review |
| June 1997 to October 1997 | Six public hearings and three public workshops |
| October 1997 | Planning Commission recommends City Council approval |
| January 1998 | City Council approves New Model Colony General Plan Amendment |
| November 1999 | New Model Colony is annexed to city of Ontario |
| December 1999 | Environmental groups file California Environmental Quality Act challenge |
| November 2001 | City and environmental groups reach settlement agreement |
| September 2002 | City Council approves master plans for NMC infrastructure |
| June 2003 | City Council approves impact fee schedule for the NMC |

*Source: City of Ontario.*

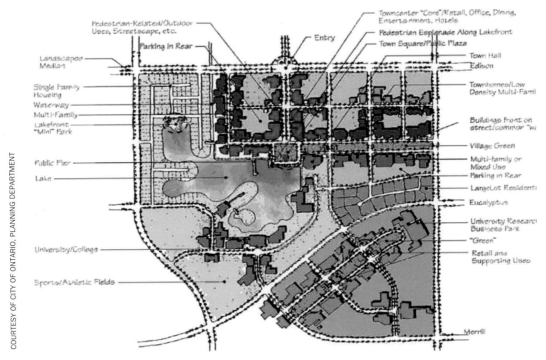

The New Model Colony General Plan calls for the town center to serve the cultural and public life of the area's residents.

include the creation of a community with a variety of uses on a grid street system with a strong sense of place. They would achieve this vision with housing on small lots, high-quality architecture, and extensive public amenities. After numerous public hearings and workshops, the city council approved the New Model Colony General Plan Amendment in January 1998, and the NMC was annexed in November 1999.

Immediately after the city council annexed the NMC, environmental groups filed a California Environmental Quality Act (CEQA) lawsuit that would last two years.[2] Eventually, the city and the environmental groups reached a settlement agreement out of court. The city of Ontario's planning director notes, "We should have engaged these groups early on, because once they saw and truly understood our plans they got on board, and now

the local environmental community sees the NMC as a paradigm for new development."

The planned infrastructure for the NMC is estimated to cost over $500 million. As noted previously, the financing of public facilities in the NMC had to adhere to the city council's clear direction and commitment that new development was to pay for itself and that existing residents in the rest of Ontario would not have to pay for infrastructure in the NMC. The burden of funding would fall on the development community. The city recommended the development community devise a mechanism on which they could all agree. As a result, a private consortium of 14 builders formed the NMC Builders LLC to finance the upfront infrastructure needs of the NMC.

The financing mechanism is a threefold system comprising (a) capital contributions through the

NMC Builders LLC, (b) impact fees, and (c) Community Facilities Districts. The developers in each Specific Plan area of the NMC are responsible for capital contributions through the private consortium. These builders are granted a credit against the development impact fee schedule. This system allows builders to offset some of their initial capital contributions.

## Effect of the New Model Colony

Although it will be 30 years until the New Model Colony is fully built out, the initial groundwork achieved to date is significant. Nine Specific Plan applications have been submitted to the city for review. Edenglen held its grand opening in April 2007 and exemplifies the planning principles and development concepts inherent in the NMC General Plan: a variety of housing types with a public amenity package oriented toward the pedestrian (see "Featured Development"). Containing more than 2,700 acres (1,092.65 hectares) of land, the additional eight SPs currently under review will lead to the development of over 10,000 single-family homes and more than 4,500 multifamily units. The

public facilities planned for these SP areas include more than 200 acres (80.94 hectares) of parks and trails and five elementary schools, one middle school, and one high school.

## Lessons Learned

In planning for the development of an 8,200-acre (3,318.42-hectare) area, the various stakeholders involved offer several keys to success, including the following:

- Planning and funding infrastructure is a necessity and often takes longer than anticipated. Be creative and think outside the box.

- Collaboration and creating a *common vision* shared by all stakeholders is a key to success. At the same time, with a buildout of 30 years, a vision should not be static but should be allowed to evolve over time.

- The city council's early and unified support early in the process was crucial to the New Model Colony's success.

- Engage community groups as early as possible.

Compactly built on a traditional grid pattern, homes at Edenglen are situated on narrow lots and have minimal front setbacks.

COURTESY OF CITY OF ONTARIO, PLANNING DEPARTMENT

# Featured Development: Edenglen

Edenglen is the first community to open within Ontario's New Model Colony. The community is a collaboration of two builders: Brookfield Homes and Standard Pacific Homes. The grand opening was held in April 2007. As outlined in the Edenglen Specific Plan, the community is pedestrian oriented, with a variety of housing types that blend and parkways, sidewalks, and community amenities. The residential neighborhoods are built on a street grid system that focuses around a centrally located park and clubhouse.

The community covers 160 acres (64.75 hectares) and features 542 homes, including 277 single-family and 307 multifamily residences. Edenglen is grouped into five neighborhoods with a range of housing types that include garden court condominiums, attached townhomes, and detached single-family residences. In addition to the housing, Edenglen will eventually support 20 acres (8.09 hectares) of commercial and 40 acres (16.19 hectares) of business park and light industrial uses. As indicated in Table 4, the density of the housing will range from 4.9 to 16 dwelling units per acre.

As Brian Geis, the vice president of Brookfield Homes Southland, notes: "The city planning staff was our biggest partner; we shared the same vision.

The first community built within Ontario's New Model Colony, Edenglen incorporates public spaces to encourage pedestrian activity.

This would not have happened if the planning director, city manager, and planning commission weren't behind the same vision." With the exception of Veranda, all the housing at Edenglen is alley loaded, with the garages moved to the rear to place an emphasis on the pedestrian. According to Geis: "At Edenglen we did not want to do a large lot program that lacks imagination. To us, the opportunity to create density meant a walkable community with

## Table 4: EDENGLEN HOUSING DENSITIES

| Neighborhood | Type | Home Size (Square Feet) | Lot Size (Square Feet) | Density (Dwelling Units per Acre) |
|---|---|---|---|---|
| Veranda | Detached | 3,600 to 4,000 | 5,000 | 4.9 |
| Gate House | Detached | 3,200 to 3,600 | 4,500 | 6.1 |
| Cottages | Detached | 1,200 to 2,000 | 3,200 | 11.2 |
| Portico | Attached | 1,800 to 2,200 | Not Applicable | 12.0 |
| Belcourt | Attached | 1,054 to 1,761 | Not Applicable | 16.0 |

a traditional grid layout and well-designed alleys to promote a pedestrian-friendly environment." Another key decision was not to gate the community to avoid making the area an island separate from the rest of the city.

The site plan supports pedestrian activity in a variety of ways, such as traffic-calming techniques, lot orientation, well-designed alleys, and generous public amenities. Traffic-calming techniques at Edenglen include narrow streets to slow vehicular traffic and make street crossing easier for pedestrians. The individual lots have minimized front setbacks and include large front balconies to promote community interaction.

The alleys within Edenglen are designed as "small streets" with attention to architectural details and landscaping. For example, the fencing along the alleyways is low enough so that residents are able to monitor the alleys visually rather than creating a blank wall.

Pinheiro Park serves as Edenglen's central park. The key features of Pinheiro Park include a central park area, clubhouse, swimming pool, outdoor amphitheater, playgrounds and tot lots, basketball half courts, outdoor dining areas, a community rose garden, and walking trails. The outdoor amphitheater will host outdoor movie nights and other community events.

The compact site design allowed the developer to dedicate a larger proportion of the land to Pinheiro Park, the central open space at Edenglen.

Edenglen site plan.

In addition to the aesthetic benefits of the pedestrian-oriented site plan, the compact land use plan was driven by the need to make the project financially feasible. To finance the infrastructure ($500 million) necessary, a certain number of units were needed.

---

2. CEQA is a state environmental disclosure law that allows citizen groups to appeal project approvals. The settlement agreement included $220 million dedicated to the purchase of sensitive environmental land in the nearby Chino basin.

# Columbia Pike Form-Based Code, Arlington County, Virginia

Arlington County, Virginia, is known throughout the United States for its corridor planning and encouragement of transit-oriented development. The Rosslyn-Ballston corridor (along Wilson Boulevard), with its high densities and mix of uses, has become a national model for older suburbs. Yet other parts of the county, particularly those not served by Metrorail, have not experienced such rapid modernization. Columbia Pike, one of southern Arlington's main east-west conduits, is one example. The three-and-a-half-mile (5.63-km) road, which runs from the Pentagon to the Fairfax County line, is a mix of strip commercial uses and aging garden apartments.

In 1986, local residents and business owners who hoped to stem disinvestment along the corridor formed the Columbia Pike Revitalization Organization (CPRO). By 1998, revitalization efforts were still slow along the Pike, so CPRO worked with Arlington County on visioning processes and designating revitalization districts along the Pike. During this process, a refined plan evolved in 2002 through efforts by CPRO, local residents, and Arlington County. The following year, the county board codified a number of key elements through the Columbia Pike Special Revitalization District Form-Based Code. The code, a new zoning tool, regulates land development by setting clear controls on building form and, to some extent, uses to create an attractive and balanced mix of private and public space. The original zoning designations are still maintained, and developers do not have to comply with the code, but the county offers incentives, such as expedited review and tax increment financing, to encourage its use. Since inception of the form-based code, a majority of the development proposals on Columbia Pike have used it. Though certainly, for both developers and residents, Arlington County's experiment with form-based code has succeeded in jump-starting Columbia Pike's revitalization.

*For more information:*
Arlington County's Columbia Pike Initiative background and reports:
http://www.arlingtonva.us/Departments/CPHD/
    Forums/columbiaCPHDForumsColumbia
    ColumbiaPikeInitiativeMain.aspx
Columbia Pike Revitalization Organization:
    http://www.columbiapikepartnership.com

*Contact information:*
Department of Community Planning,
    Housing and Development
Planning Division
#1 Courthouse Plaza
2100 Clarendon Boulevard, Suite 700
Arlington, VA 22201
703-228-3825

## Community Information

Arlington County, Virginia, is an older, established inner suburb located across the Potomac River from Washington, D.C. Arlington is known for its high-quality public schools, quaint neighborhoods, and easy access to Washington via the Metrorail system. From 2000 to early 2007, Arlington's population grew an estimated 7 percent to 202,800; it is among the most densely populated jurisdictions in the United States, with about 7,860 people per square mile.

Arlington's housing stock is composed of mostly multifamily housing (60 percent) and has seen a slight decline in the percentage of single-family homes, both attached and detached, as singles and childless couples are increasingly drawn to the county. The bulk of Arlington's single-family homes were built during the World War II era, and many of those neighborhoods have become ethnic enclaves. In 2005, about 35 percent of Arlington County's residents were Hispanic/Latino, African American, Asian, or multiracial, and almost one-quarter of residents were born outside the United States.

The 26-square-mile (67.34-square-km) county grew from predominantly a bedroom community in the 1940s to a regional economic engine with over a million square feet (92,903 square meters) of office space. The county's biggest employer is the federal government, but it also hosts several prominent private sector companies, such as Lockheed Martin, Marriott International, and US Airways. Part of Arlington's draw to employers is its highly educated workforce; in 2005, slightly more than 66 percent of adults 25 years of age and older had at least a bachelor's degree and about 36 percent had a graduate or professional degree. The 2007 median household income was $84,800.

## Neighborhood Information

Columbia Pike is one of Arlington's main east-west roadways and serves as a commuter road that funnels residents into job centers such as the Pentagon, downtown Washington, D.C., and the Skyline area in Fairfax County. The Pike is often referred to as "South Arlington's Main Street." Despite the centrality of Columbia Pike, it has experienced a steady economic downturn. Columbia Pike's troubles began during the planning for the Washington Metro in the 1960s, when Arlington County chose to run its Metrorail lines to the north and east of Columbia Pike. The Orange line ran along the then economically depressed Wilson Boulevard corridor, while the Blue line traveled south from the Pentagon to

National Airport. The Orange line was also convenient to the new Interstate 66, an interstate highway and major infrastructure investment. Without rail and the investment that often comes with it, Columbia Pike stalled economically. Reinvestment did not occur, and retail, business development, and housing stagnated.

Columbia Pike is slowly experiencing a renaissance and is now a bohemian mix of authentically retro diners and movie theaters, auto dealerships, ethnic restaurants, strip centers, and apartment buildings. The area's main promoter, the Columbia Pike Revitalization Organization, hosts an annual blues festival and a seasonal farmers market and advertises Columbia Pike's offbeat retail and cultural diversity. Columbia Pike residents asked for and received improved bus service; the county and a group of residents and business owners are hoping to build light rail in the corridor. The current bus service is the most highly used public bus line in the state, with more than 11,000 daily boardings.

## Government Structure

A five-member county board, with an appointed county manager, oversees Arlington County. The county board members are elected at large for staggered four-year terms. The board makes general policy decisions for all county government functions, which the county manager administers (for example, public safety, trash collection, parks and recreation, libraries). The board sets real estate, personal property, and other tax rates and establishes the work program for the county by adopting an annual budget. The board makes all land use and zoning decisions within the limitations imposed by the Code of Virginia. It oversees transportation policies related to such issues as widening, narrowing, and repairing of county streets, sidewalks, and bicycle trails. Arlington does not contain any incorporated cities and therefore does not have any mayors. A wide network of civic organizations and homeowners associations work directly with the county's government departments.

The Department of Community Planning, Housing and Development is one of 12 departments reporting to the county manager. It is responsible for permitting, zoning, code enforcement, housing policy, general planning, and neighborhood services. The planning department will typically work with community residents and development experts to formulate plans that are eventually brought before the county board for approval. Arlington County residents are encouraged to participate and comment on proposed projects, which are profiled on the county's Web site.

## Policy Enactment

To prevent further economic distress, Columbia Pike business owners banded together in 1986 to form CPRO. The county created the Revitalization District and allocated bond funding for streetscape improvements. In 1998, CPRO worked closely with the Arlington County planning department to establish the Columbia Pike Initiative, which was approved by the Arlington County Board. The initiative, which focused on revitalizing the eastern section of Columbia Pike, was so well received that the community and the county began a visioning process for the redevelopment of the entire corridor. In 2002, and after hundreds of community meetings, the collaboration bore fruit in a long-range vision and plan that focused on economic development, land use and zoning, urban design, transportation, public infrastructure, and open space and recreational needs. Also in 2002,

the county board adopted the collaborative effort now known as *The Columbia Pike Initiative—A Revitalization Plan.*

After the adoption of the revitalization plan, the community participated in an intensive charrette in the fall of 2002 that produced specific design recommendations that became the basis of the Columbia Pike Special Revitalization District Form-Based Code, which the county adopted in early 2003. The form-based code was a direct solution to many of the problems identified during the charrette: entitlement delays, uncertainty in the approval process, lack of pedestrian access, and obvious visual blight in the corridor. The form-based code would make the development process simpler, shorter, and more predictable. Without the code, economic development along Columbia Pike would have been almost impossible. To date,

Arlington County's form-based code regulates land use along Columbia Pike by controlling building orientation, height, and form.

COURTESY OF LAWRENCE LUK

CPRO and residents have been satisfied with the plan and the current development projects approved under the new code.

When the form-based code was adopted, questions were still unresolved regarding the width, design, and use of street space along Columbia Pike. At that time, the county board established the Columbia Pike Street Space Planning Task Force to consider those issues and develop streetscape recommendations for the length of the Pike. The task force included representatives from civic associations near the Pike, as well as representatives from various county advisory groups and commissions. The task force met for nearly a year, and in February 2004, the county board accepted the *Columbia Pike Street Space Planning Task Force Report*. The board subsequently adopted various Master Transportation Plan amendments recommended in the report, including the street cross sections. The ultimate goal is to remake the corridor into a "main street," geared to pedestrians, bicyclists, and transit riders as well as motorists. The Columbia Pike Initiative Plan was also updated in 2005 to review the program that had been made and to discuss changes in course, such as the adoption of the form-based code.

## Program Details

Form-based codes are relatively new planning tools. Originally, they were sets of instructions for developers to use on greenfield sites. The codes then became efficient ways of handling inner-city redevelopment when hundreds of property owners were involved. They regulate the key aspects of urban form, such as the height of buildings, how close structures are to the street, and how windows and doors should face public spaces. Form-based codes make streets and buildings work together to create a desirable public realm and subsequently add value to surrounding properties. Form-based codes can be confused with design guidelines but have a separate purpose. In most cases, form-based codes regulate the general footprint of a building, not its actual style. Moreover, developers and the public, who helped define the codes, are put at ease with the certainty provided by form-based codes,

The Columbia Pike form-based code is incentive based, encouraging developers to preserve historic features in exchange for height bonuses.

and in turn, certainty provides less opposition and expedited review.

The Columbia Pike Form-Based Code (CPFBC) is a legal, yet optional, document that regulates land development by setting controls on building form to create optimal public space and mixed-use development. The CPFBC uses illustrations and specific parameters for height, siting, and building elements to address the necessities for redevelopment as envisioned by the public. The code applies to development within four revitalization nodes, all encompassing one segmented district along the Pike, and uses maps to indicate what type of building can be erected at any location within a district.

Developers who choose to use the CPFBC can expect an expedited formal approval process that takes between 30 and 60 days. A project with a property under 40,000 square feet (3,716 square meters) and a building footprint under 30,000 square feet (2,787 square meters) may submit for approval through the 30-day by-right option process, which involves no mandated public hearings. For projects over the square-foot maximums, the code requires a 55-day special exception/use permit option. This process involves public hearings before the county planning commission and the county board. Developers who opt for use of the CPFBC within the revitalization district are eligible for county incentives, such as technology tax credits, rehabilitation tax exemptions, and tax increment financing for public infrastructure.

The CPFBC specifically addresses blocks and alleys, building envelope standards, streetscape, parking, primary and secondary retail uses, historic preservation, building materials, and public improvements.

**Under construction, Siena Park will replace an aging grocery store along Columbia Pike. Each facade includes a primary entrance to the building, as required by the form-based code.**

VIEW FROM ADAMS STREET

Code highlights include the following:

- All lots must share a frontage line with the street by means of a required building line.
- Alleys must provide access to the rear of all lots, and curb cuts are limited to no more than one per 200 feet (60.96 meters) of street frontage.
- Maximum building floor plate is 30,000 square feet (2,787 square meters); beyond that limit, a special exception is necessary, except for grocery stores, which are allowed up to 50,000 square feet (4,645 square meters).
- Each facade should include a functioning, primary street entry to the building.
- Street trees must be planted at the time of development and spaced 25 to 30 feet (7.62 to 9.14 meters) on center.
- The developer is responsible for the installation of streetlights on its side of the street.
- The developer, at the time of construction, should install sidewalks with a minimum six-foot-wide (1.83-meter-wide) "clear zone" of smooth concrete.
- Parking should be located at convenient locations with reduced single-purpose reserved parking and maximized on-street parking.
- Bicycle parking is mandatory.
- Bonus height is given for preservation of historic properties and facades.

## Effect of the CPFBC

For the most part, developers and the public have responded positively to the CPFBC. Arlington County has since added seven amendments to the plan to clarify certain aspects and has been working through unforeseen kinks as they are encountered. The plan has attracted national media attention and has resulted in increased bus service ("PikeRide") and, as hoped, an increase in redevelopment activity. The U.S. Air Force recently built a dramatic memorial at the eastern end of Columbia Pike, providing a dramatic gateway to the development efforts, and Columbia Pike residents, the county, and area businesses are working to bring light-rail service to the area.

Since the inception of form-based codes, projects totaling more than $500 million have been approved or are in the approval process. They include townhomes and several mixed-use developments, as well as a new grocery store with a residential component and Halstead @ Columbia Pike (see "Featured Development").

## Lessons Learned

As with all innovations, people need time to become familiar and comfortable with form-based codes. Drafting a form-based code requires discussions with attorneys in the jurisdiction and with zoning administrators to confirm wording and enforceability. Time must also be allowed for planning staff to work with other departments and staff in the jurisdiction—including building code officials, and traffic and transportation planners and engineers—to educate them on the new code.

Adopters of form-based codes must also understand the effect the code may have on the environment. To this end, it is necessary to develop test-case scenarios that use outside architectural or planning assistance. It is also important to conduct a survey of existing streets, curblines, centerlines, and utilities.

## Featured Development: Halstead @ Columbia Pike

The first project to be approved within Arlington County's form-based code effort is the Halstead @ Columbia Pike, an $85 million development with 269 apartments and 42,350 square feet (3,934 square meters) of retail, including 7,500 square feet (697 square meters) for a free medical clinic. The site is located at a major intersection along Columbia Pike and required the demolition of an outmoded power substation and the restoration of the historic Arlington Hardware facade. Halstead @ Columbia Pike will include 450 underground parking spaces; Arlington County will provide 128 parking stalls that will be available to the public.

The project will feature a new U-shaped complex, combining shops, condominiums, and shared parking. A pedestrian walkway through the complex will provide convenient access to stores, parking, and the street, as well as to transit options. The Arlington Free Clinic will own its own condominium retail space, giving it a permanent home and enabling it to provide needed free and low-cost medical services to Arlington residents in the long term.

A mixed-use project, Halstead @ Columbia Pike fulfills the vision of the form-based code as a cornerstone of the "main street" concept by preserving and enhancing the streetscape. The "main street" is achieved through a lively mix of shop fronts, sidewalk cafés, and other commercial uses at street level, overlooked by canopy shade trees and upper-story residences and offices.

The first project approved under Arlington's new form-based code, the Halstead @ Columbia Pike is a cornerstone of Columbia Pike's revitalization efforts.

COURTESY OF DSF ADVISORS

COURTESY OF DSF ADVISORS

As envisioned by the form-based code, this project provides shared parking. The developer and the county are jointly funding the 128 shared parking spaces. These spaces will be available to the public 24 hours a day, seven days a week. In addition, the Halstead project is convenient to a number of bicycle trails and routes. On-street bike lanes are proposed for most of Columbia Pike, and the developer is providing 62 bike-storage spaces and ten sidewalk bike racks. The project is due for completion in 2008.

# Downtown Zoning Changes, Seattle, Washington

Major revisions to Seattle's downtown zoning code were enacted in April 2006. They set the stage for dramatically increasing the density of downtown Seattle, and they support regional planning efforts to curtail sprawl and make better use of resources. The zoning changes, which cover most of the area within three downtown "neighborhoods," are a major step in realizing the goals of Seattle's framework Comprehensive Plan of 1994.

*For more information:*

http://www.seattle.gov/DPD/Planning/Downtown_
Zoning_Changes/Overview/

*Contact information:*

Diane Sugimura
Director, Department of Planning and
Development
City of Seattle
700 5th Ave., Suite 2000
P.O. Box 34019
Seattle, WA 98124-4019
Diane.sugimura@seattle.gov
206-233-3882

## Community Information

The population of the city of Seattle was approaching 580,000 as of 2007. It is the largest city in a metropolitan area of well over 3.5 million in western Washington, along the shores of Elliott Bay and the Puget Sound. A magnet for growth, the city has added about 4,000 residents per year for the last 16 years, and the upward population trend is expected to accelerate. The city has a goal of reducing sprawl in the region by accepting a large share of its population increase. The Seattle area, historic home of Weyerhaeuser and Boeing, is now also the home of Microsoft, Starbucks, and Immunex.

## Neighborhood Information

The area directly affected by the zoning changes is 500 acres (202.34 hectares), roughly half of the 950 acres (384.45 hectares) in Seattle's downtown area. It includes the commercial core, government centers, and the financial district. It also includes growing residential neighborhoods on the edges of Belltown and in the Denny Triangle. To the north of these is the booming South Lake Union area and to the south is Pioneer Square, the International District, historic stations (now emerging as multimodal centers), and baseball and football stadiums. The area is bounded by Interstate 5 on the east and by Pike Place Market and historic waterfront to the west. It contains many cultural assets, including the Seattle Art Museum, Benaroya Hall (Seattle Symphony), and historic theaters.

With the 2006 downtown zoning code changes, Seattle has embraced much more density downtown by raising height limits.

## Political Structure

Seattle has a mayor-council form of government, all elected to four-year terms in at-large, nonpartisan races. The mayor and the nine-member council are well balanced in power, negotiating sometimes from opposing positions. A strong consensus exists among city officials about the importance of environmental issues. Land use legislation, including zoning changes, is typically studied by city staff and proposed by the mayor. Other departments may be involved, but land use policies are centered in the Department of Planning and Development, which includes strategic planning. After the mayor proposes zoning changes, the city council and its staff independently study, modify, and enact them. Each branch of government may conduct its own public outreach and community involvement process.

## Major Features of the Downtown Zoning Changes

Seattle's new downtown zoning code redraws the boundaries of some zones. The changes are expected to have a major effect upon the future of the downtown office core, a portion of Belltown and the Denny Triangle to the north, and a small part of the retail core. They will change the profile of downtown Seattle, incrementally shifting density northward. Following are the major features of the code.

**Height.** The zoning changes increase floor/area ratio (FAR) and height for commercial uses and increase height for residential uses. The most significant height change is inside the expanded boundaries of the downtown mixed commercial (DMC) zones, up from the previous allowance of 125 to 240 feet (38.10 to 73.15 meters) to a new allowance of 440 feet (134.11 meters), including 10 percent bonus height for certain design features. Of the five zones included in the zoning code revisions, four have three successive height limits

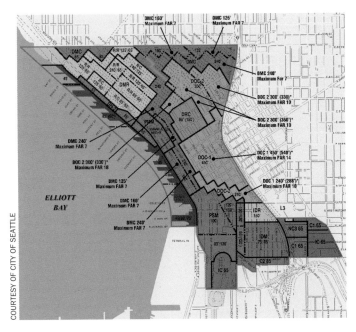

COURTESY OF CITY OF SEATTLE

Prior to the zoning changes in 2006, Seattle's zoning map (above) imposed lower height limits in the downtown area. The new downtown zoning map (below) dramatically raises height limits for residential uses, and floor/area ratios in commercial zones.

COURTESY OF CITY OF SEATTLE

based on type of use and bonus provisions. Where the zones listed below have more than one height limit, the first is for nonresidential uses, the second is for residential uses not using bonuses, and the third represents a bonus height limit for residential uses to be granted in return for contributions to affordable housing and for meeting other standards of performance ("U" stands for unlimited):

- Downtown Mixed Commercial 1 (DMC1): 160 feet (48.77 meters)
- Downtown Mixed Commercial 2 (DMC2): 240, 290, 400 feet (73.15, 88.39, 121.92 meters)
- Downtown Mixed Commercial 3 (DMC3): 340, 290, 400 feet (103.63, 88.39, 121.92 meters)
- Downtown Office Commercial (DOC1): U, 450 feet (137.16 meters), U
- Downtown Office Commercial 2 (DOC2): 500, 300, 500 feet (152.40, 91.44, 152.40 meters)

**Floor/Area Ratio.** In the amended code, the density of nonresidential land uses continues to be limited by FAR. FAR is the ratio of floor area per lot area, excluding below-grade areas. The basic FAR is five in DMC and DOC2 zones and six in DOC1. Any additional (bonus) FAR in the project is awarded through special provisions. The ranges in two sections of the downtown office core are five to 14 and six to 20, from base to maximum (bonus) FAR. Heights in the same zones range from 500 feet (152.40 meters) to unlimited. In two mixed commercial zones, nonresidential buildings are limited to 240 feet (73.15 meters) and 340 feet (103.63 meters), while residential towers can rise to 440 feet (134.11 meters) with bonuses, about 38 stories of habitable area.

**Office and Commercial Bonus Development.** In DOC2, the first .75 FAR above the base obligates the developer to achieve Leadership in Energy and Environmental Design (LEED) Silver certification for the project. The LEED increment in DOC1 is

1.0 above the base. Additional FAR, up to a maximum of 20 FAR in the DOC zone, is subject to bonus contributions directed at two categories of public benefits. The first is affordable housing and child care (which can add 75 percent bonus FAR). This requirement may be satisfied by including these elements in the development, by developing them on an adjacent property, or by contributing to a fund at a rate of $22 per square foot toward affordable housing in the downtown urban center. The second is nonhousing benefits (which can add 25 percent of bonus FAR). These include contributions to a slate of civic and cultural projects, such as open space and landmark theaters, as illustrated in Table 5, which shows how bonus floor area is proposed to be gained in actual projects.

**Residential Bonus Development.** For residential projects, bonus height is achieved in the following ways (see Table 6):

*Affordable housing:* To reach the applicable bonus height limits, affordable housing may be built into the project or on an adjacent lot (performance option). Low- and moderate-income housing must be provided that is equal to 11 percent of the bonus development area. Alternatively, a contribution can be made to an affordable housing fund administered by the city (payment option) averaging $18.95 per square foot of bonus development. A combination of these two options can be negotiated.

*LEED rating:* Bonus height also requires a LEED Silver rating from the U.S. Green Building Council. Failure to achieve this threshold rating at buildout will result in a land use code violation and prorated penalty.

*Rooftop amenities:* The maximum applicable height for residential use may be increased by 10 percent in the DMC zones for rooftop features and residential amenity spaces.

**Street-Level Requirements.** Special provisions in the code are intended to activate the streetscape and contribute to the pedestrian realm. They include the following:

*Frontage:* On streets requiring street-level use, base frontage must be composed of retail, child care, customer service office, entertainment, museum, library, or public atrium space, and these uses must be within ten feet (3.05 meters) of the property line or abut a public open space.

*Parking in structures:* The code contains complex restrictions on above-grade parking to minimize the negative impact of parking structures on the pedestrian environment. Parking at and above grade that is inside structures is covered by a number of provisions intended to protect the pedestrian environment from visual blight. On designated major pedestrian streets, parking uses in structures must be separated from the street by other uses at street level. On less-important

### Table 5: BONUS CONTRIBUTIONS FROM NEW COMMERCIAL PROJECTS

| Project | Zoning Code | Site Area (Sq. Ft.) | Total Chargeable Floor Area (Sq. ft.) | Base FAR; Floor Area (Sq. ft.) | LEED Incentive FAR; Floor Area (Sq. ft.) | 25 Percent Nonhousing Bonus/Transferable Development Right (TDR) Options | 75 Percent Housing/Child Care Options |
|---|---|---|---|---|---|---|---|
| **West 8th** 2001 8th Ave | DOC2 | 34,521 | 465,548 | 5; 172,605 | 0.75; 25,891 | 2 FAR (71,194 sq. ft.)<br>• 35,597 sq. ft. (1 FAR) major performing arts theater TDR (required)<br>• 35,597 sq. ft. (1 FAR) within-block TDR from Fare Start lot | 5.6 FAR (195,859 sq. ft.)<br>• 112,175 sq. ft. (3.2 FAR) housing/child care bonus contribution ($2.5 million)<br>• 83,684 sq. ft. (2.4 FAR) housing TDR ($1.2 million for 58,859 sq. ft.) |
| **1918 8th Ave** | DOC2 | 26,032 | 364,123* | 5; 130,160 | 0.75; 19,524 | 2 FAR (53,366 sq. ft.)<br>• 26,846 sq. ft. (1 FAR) major performing arts theater TDR (required) | 6.2 FAR (161,073 sq. ft.)<br>• Approximately $3.5 million if provided through contribution to housing/child care fund |
| **810 Western** | DMC 160 | 23,980 | 167,860 | 5; 119,900 | 0.25; 5,995 | 0.25 FAR (5,995 sq. ft.)<br>• Green street setback and improvements<br>• Major performing arts theater TDR (required) | 1.5 FAR (35,970 sq. ft.)<br>• Approximately $791,340 through contribution to housing/child care fund |
| **TOTAL** | | | 997,531 | 422,665 | 51,410 | 65,441 sq. ft. major performing arts theater TDR<br>35,597 sq. ft. within-block TDR<br>2,998 sq. ft. green street<br>**104,036 sq. ft. total** | $6.8 million housing/child care fund<br>$1.2 million housing TDR<br>**$8.0 million total** |

*Source: City of Seattle, Department of Planning and Development.*

*Contribution to preservation of Julie Apartments across the street from site, specified as public benefit for combined lot development (23.49.041). This project is a combined lot development and may ultimately have more floor area.

pedestrian streets, parking must be separated by other uses on at least 30 percent of the frontage, and the part that is exposed must be screened and enhanced by some combination of architectural detailing, artwork, and landscaping. For small lots (less than 30,000 square feet [2,787 square meters] or 150 feet [45.72 meters] in depth), in-structure parking is allowed up to four stories above street level, provided that an equal number of parking levels are below grade. This standard can be partially waived as long as maximum feasible below-grade parking is provided. On larger lots, all parking levels above street level must be separated from the street by another use.

**Upper-Level Development Standards.** To preserve light and views, the code distinguishes between a tower and a base in downtown buildings. In residential structures, the tower is the part above 65 feet (19.81 meters), with a maximum height of 290 feet (88.39 meters) in a nonbonus project and 400 feet (121.92 meters) for a bonus project in the DMC zone. The net effect of the upper-level

development standards is that towers that do not exceed the base height limit have average residential gross floor plate area limits of 10,000 square feet (929 square meters) with limits on tower width. Bonus-height towers have maximum average residential gross floor plate area limits of 10,700 square feet (994 square meters). The maximum floor size permitted above 65 feet (19.81 meters) is 11,500 square feet (1,068 square meters).

To protect views along the streets that run perpendicular to the waterfront in the DMC zones—Seattle's "slot views"—the regulations limit tower widths in most cases to 120 feet (36.58 meters) along the avenues, with more-detailed adjustments for differing lot sizes and conditions. In DOC zones on large sites, above 240 feet (73.15 meters), the tower width is limited to 145 feet (44.20 meters). Minimum tower spacing in DMC zones varies according to the neighborhood.

Upper-level setbacks are required near the Pike Place Market Historical District to reflect the existing heights. A setback of 15 feet (4.57 meters)

## Table 6: BONUS CONTRIBUTIONS FROM NEW RESIDENTIAL PROJECTS

| Project | Zoning Code | Number of Units | Contribution |
|---|---|---|---|
| 1521 2nd Avenue | DMC 240/290-400 | Under construction 143 units | 97,467 sq. ft. bonus floor area ($1.75 million housing contribution) |
| 2000 3rd Avenue | DMC 240/290-400 | Permitted 431 units | 107,030 sq. ft. bonus floor area gained through contribution to YWCA |
| Olive 8 1635 8th Avenue | DOC2 500/300-500 | Under construction 231 units | Top three floors only 37,635 sq. ft. bonus floor area ($570,000 housing contribution) |
| 2301 6th Avenue | DMC 240/290-400 | Permit application 646 units | 179,356 sq. ft. bonus floor area in two towers (estimated $3.6 million total over two phases) |
| TOTAL | | 1,451 units | |

*Source: City of Seattle, Department of Planning and Development.*

is required above 65 feet (19.81 meters). Setbacks are required above 45 feet (13.72 meters) on a designated green street. Upper-level setbacks are also required along designated view corridors.

**Common Recreation Space.** Zoning regulations require common recreational space for new residential developments, in an amount no less than 5 percent of the total gross floor area in residential use. Half of it may be enclosed, and it may be on top of buildings that are at the maximum bonus height limit. Contributing to abutting green streets will reduce the requirement by half.

**Departures.** A board specially appointed for the downtown area grants zoning code departures through a process of design review. Under the amended code, only a narrow list of provisions, including height and density limits and view corridor setbacks, are not subject to departure. More latitude is now possible through design review if the overall intentions of the code are served.

## Overall Planning

The city of Seattle has been very forward-thinking. Its planning policies and the changes to the downtown zoning code are just one part of a citywide effort to implement smart growth policies. For many years, the city has sought to achieve a wide range of smart growth goals, such as encouraging higher densities, creating greater connectivity between neighborhoods, developing mixed-income and mixed-use communities, and providing and preserving open space. Beginning in the early 1990s under Mayor Norm Rice, Seattle embarked on an overall planning process intended to complement regional growth

management goals. These goals, which have state backing in Washington's Growth Management Act of 1990, include much greater densities in urbanized areas and the protection of rural and wild lands from suburban-type development.

Recast by Mayor Greg Nickels in 2005, the goals of the then-proposed zoning changes were neatly summarized in the phrase "livable downtown Seattle." The mayor reflected a growing understanding of the benefits of density along with his own goal of attracting a critical mass of downtown residents whose 24-hour presence would bring greater security and opportunity to the neighborhoods there. The recently adopted changes will help accommodate a doubling of downtown residential density in 20 years, from

The city of Seattle used axonometric models to explore the possible buildout options after the downtown zoning changes.

20,000 to about 40,000 residents, as well as up to 17.9 million square feet (1,662,964 square meters) in new commercial space. The changes are designed to increase the attractiveness of residential and mixed-use development in the downtown commercial core and peripheral mixed-use zones.

Written into the downtown zoning changes are several strategies that serve the following goals:

**Density.** The downtown Seattle zoning changes dramatically increase density by lifting height limits in a number of contiguous downtown zones and increasing FAR in others. For commercial development under the bonus system, maximum FARs are more than twice the base FARs (as previously described).

**Connectivity.** The downtown Seattle area is a regional center and evolving transit hub, where automobile traffic must be managed and pedestrians increasingly accommodated. The most significant increases in commercial density are in office core areas along the light-rail alignment, for maximum commuter convenience. Encouraging the use of transit and nonautomobile transportation, such as bicycles and walking, is an important part of the height and FAR bonus system. It rewards developers for dedicating private land and capital to pedestrian amenities, such as a hill climb assist, a hillside terrace, plazas, public atriums, or green street improvements. In addition, transit system accommodations such as station access easements and improved access to station mezzanines can be traded for extra FAR. A network of designated green streets also helps emphasize pedestrian connections between neighborhoods.

**Mix of Uses.** The downtown zoning changes encourage mixed-use and residential development by creating important opportunities for residential towers in areas that have previously been primarily reserved for the expansion of commercial and office use. To encourage storefront retail, the city requires street-level uses on a mapped network of street frontages, and the floor area occupied by these uses is exempt from FAR calculations throughout downtown. Because of these measures and the pedestrian amenities that the code also supports, downtown Seattle should achieve a more desirable balance of residential development and other uses.

**Mixed Income and Affordability.** Downtown Seattle has seen an influx of luxury towers over the last five years and a dramatic decrease in low-income housing over the last four decades, a decrease that has been somewhat stemmed over the last two decades by low-income housing preservation and development. The bonus system applied to new development will help further balance the housing mix. Bonus contributions based on the amended downtown code are projected to yield a return of over $100 million in today's dollars for affordable housing and child care over the next 20 years. The Department of Housing will manage the proceeds, providing a grant fund for members of Seattle's strong nonprofit housing community.

In the base of Fifteen Twenty-One Second Avenue, work/studio units help activate the pedestrian corridor.

COURTESY OF OPUS N.W./THE JUSTEN COMPANY

**Open Space and Parks.** No additional land is set aside for open space as a part of the downtown zoning changes. However, the changes include provisions for securing open space in the future. Development rights can be transferred from public open-space sites to help fund their acquisition and improvement as parks. Commercial development can gain part of the floor area allowed above the base FAR by providing open space for public use on the project site. Because 5 percent of the gross residential square footage is required to be devoted to shared recreation uses that include rooftop terraces and gardens, and because the area essentially counts double if it is connected to the street at grade or just above, code changes encourage the provision of open space adjacent to the public realm. The requirement for LEED certification in connection with bonus height will encourage green roofs and rooftop gardens. Bonus FAR for open space must be accommodated as part of the 25 percent share of total bonus floor area above the LEED increment.

**Parking.** Parking requirements for downtown residential development were eliminated in 1985. In the downtown zoning changes, the requirement for parking is eliminated for commercial development also, and a maximum limit of one space per thousand square feet (92.9 square meters) is placed on the amount of parking that can be provided with office development. The design and location of parking is subject to limitations.

## Process of Enactment

Current Seattle zoning is based on title 23 of the 1985 zoning code, which was part of an effort to replace a mapped comprehensive plan with a policy catalog and new implementing zoning. The first chapters for single-family and multifamily areas were adopted in 1982 under title 23. Downtown zoning was adopted in 1985, and it included 12 separate zones in downtown Seattle, some of which matched previously established special review districts like Pioneer Square, the Pike Place Market, and the International District. Key goals of the 1985 zoning included concentrating employment near existing or planned mass transit and encouraging more residential development downtown. Height limits were set for some areas where none had previously applied, but the downtown office core had no height limits. There were extensive requirements for ground-floor retail downtown. The retail core itself was clearly defined, and bonuses and incentives were given for street parks or green street features.

In 1989, the Citizens' Alternative Plan (CAP) Initiative passed, largely in reaction to a surge in downtown high-rise development, which included the 76-story, 28 FAR Columbia Center, actually vested under pre–title 23 regulations. The initiative resulted in lowered height and density limits in three downtown zones, establishing a height limit of 450 feet (137.16 meters) in the DOC1 zone. In addition, the amount of commercial floor area that could be permitted annually was limited for a ten-year period. The CAP went into effect just as a downturn in the economy discouraged any tower construction, and nearly a decade passed before any were actually designed and constructed under the law. With modifications, the CAP remained in effect until the first phase of zoning amendments implemented neighborhood plans in 2001.

The state of Washington's Growth Management Act, passed in 1990, imposed a legal obligation to plan for limiting sprawl and protecting rural and wild lands. At the same time, Seattle began a comprehensive planning process based upon the concept of urban villages and five urban centers, including downtown. The draft plan, which set the highest density goals for the center of Seattle, was published in 1994. It became the framework for planning in more than 30 separate neighborhoods that began their own planning processes based on goals for open space, new housing, transit-oriented development, and neighborhood commercial development.

Five of those neighborhoods are considered part of downtown urban center. They joined in a provisional planning group that addressed the land use and transportation plan of 1985 and produced recommendations that were incorporated into two phases of amendments to downtown zoning in 1999 and 2001, before the changes of 2006.

In 2003, the city published a Draft Environmental Impact Statement analyzing the effects of proposed height and density increases on traffic and transportation, views, bulk, scale, and urban form. The mayor's proposal for downtown zoning, titled *Center City Strategy* and calling for a "livable walkable Seattle, 24/7," was published in 2004 and became the preferred alternative. The final Environmental Impact Statement was published in January 2005. After extensive study and review of the preferred alternative as well as a number of revisions by the city council, final legislation for the zoning changes was enacted.

The emerging downtown Seattle skyline rises above the historic Pike Place Market.

COURTESY OF OPUS N.W./THE JUSTEN COMPANY

## Effects

Based upon economic indicators and zoning code changes, the city is on the cusp of the most rapid development of residential units in history within the boundaries of downtown Seattle. Currently, 13 projects are already under construction, and another 49 are proposed. If all of these projects are built, downtown Seattle will have more than 8,300 new residential units by 2010. By year, the actual and projected residential units coming on line in downtown Seattle are shown in Table 7.

Judging by the presales that have already occurred, the market will rapidly absorb these units, and permit applications for thousands more can be expected before the end of the current plan period in 2024. Of the units scheduled to be ready for move-in in 2009, 488 are already presold.

Interpreting sales activity in the last year, changes to the downtown zoning code seem to have added a premium on land value of approximately 20 percent in the study area. Over time, this rise in property values will negatively affect the supply of affordable housing, which contributions to housing through the bonus system may only partially mitigate.

So far under the bonus system, office and commercial projects currently under construction or largely through the permitting process are expected to generate about $8 million in contributions to housing and child care. Additional resources will be directed to nonhousing public amenities, such as performing arts theaters, green street improvements, and employment training centers.

Residential projects permitted under the code changes are expected to generate about $6 million in obligated contributions toward affordable and low-income housing.

## Lessons Learned

Seattle's downtown zoning code grows out of a decades-long shift in perceptions and policies about the center city and a vision that is shared by a broad constituency, including environmentalists and developers. It mirrors state growth management mandates to reduce sprawl and concentrate growth in urbanized areas, and it is grounded in a process that includes current downtown businesses and residents, activists and developers. For all of these reasons, there have been no politically relevant objections or challenges to the code changes after enactment.

Because the bonus calculations in the code changes are based upon the concept of "mitigation" instead of specific monetary goals for housing and amenities, assessing the success of the bonus system will be difficult. Assessing the code changes as a spur to development is also difficult to separate from other market factors. Nevertheless, since the code changes went into effect in April 2006, the

### Table 7: SEATTLE RESIDENTIAL UNITS

| Year | Units |
|------|-------|
| 2005 | 390 |
| 2006 | 47 |
| 2007 | 1,031 |
| 2008 | 1,738[a] |
| 2009 | 1,791[b] |

Source: Seattle economist Matthew Gardner.

a. Permitted under new code, with two projects of 374 units, including Fifteen Twenty-One Second Avenue, going to full bonus height.

b. Includes 200 units in projects taking advantage of bonus heights.

pace of downtown development has increased substantially, and a number of developers have chosen to take part in the bonus programs and build higher than the base limits.

As of 2007, zoning changes and market seem to be well aligned. More than 25 permit applications for downtown development have been filed under the new code, and 14 are for towers that would reach bonus height limits and yield substantial payments into the city's affordable housing fund, totaling about $14 million in obligations to contribute to affordable housing, child care centers, and other amenities. If downtown development proceeds apace, the city is very likely to reach its projection of just over $100 million in bonus funding for housing over the next two decades.

Few overall issues about the application of the code have come to the attention of the Department of Planning and Development since the adoption of the zoning code changes in April 2006, with one exception: Intended tower spacing (and resulting view corridors) can be skewed by a combination of construction timing and position on the building lot. This issue is likely to be resolved by a process of executive review within the Department of Planning and Development.

Two overarching lessons from Seattle's downtown code changes and adoption process follow:

**Flexibility can support policy objectives and maintain steady growth at the same time.** Each zone's formula for bonus height and density incentives can be tied to a number of mixed-use types, giving private developers and their design teams a wide range of choices while allowing the city to hold fast to long-term objectives for urban form, the pedestrian environment, and overall livability. This flexibility allows room for market swings in each category, increasing the likelihood of buildout and corresponding contributions to

the city's objectives. The mix of uses in the code changes has already given rise to some project types new to Seattle. Six new projects under the revised code combine a hotel with residential units, and a two-tower complex pairs residential with office-commercial uses. The reduction in design points that are not subject to departure through design review allows even more flexibility in building design.

**The private development community can directly and actively support a wide range of public amenities.** The policy objectives embodied in the code are supported by developers, investors, and downtown business owners. A general understanding exists that the pedestrian environment, long-term livability, and property value are all intertwined.

## Featured Development: Fifteen Twenty-One Second Avenue

Fifteen Twenty-One Second Avenue is a 39-story high-rise that clearly expresses Seattle's new downtown zoning code. The slim tower, located near the historic Pike Street Market, rises above a seven-story base that contains nearly 3,000 square feet of storefront retail space. Sculpted with arcing walls to maximize views from every unit, the tower contains 143 large condominiums, with move-ins beginning in the last quarter of 2008.

Located on Second Avenue between Pine and Pike streets, the midblock project takes advantage of the new bonus height limit, rising above the 240-foot (73.15-meter) base height assigned to that location to 440 feet (134.11 meters). Of the total usable approximately 273,000 feet (25,363 square meters), the top 97,467 square feet (9,055 meters) is part of the bonus height allowance based on the formula embedded in the zoning code changes. The owner will contribute $1.75 million to the city's low-income housing fund (payment option) rather than build the housing into the project or on an adjacent site (performance option).

The development of the tower is a collaboration between Minneapolis-based Opus Northwest and Samis Land Company. William Justen is managing director of Samis Land Company, founder of the Justen Company, and former director of the city of Seattle's building and planning department. The land, owned by Samis prior to development, was acquired by Opus just prior to construction. Opus Northwest is a division of the Opus Group, a $2.1 billion national real estate company specializing in large office, industrial, retail, and multifamily projects. Opus Northwest has done a variety of projects in the greater Seattle area, including the

The concourse on one side of the Fifteen Twenty-One Second Avenue tower base provides vehicular access to parking that is off Second Avenue, an important pedestrian corridor.

COURTESY OF OPUS N.W./THE JUSTEN COMPANY

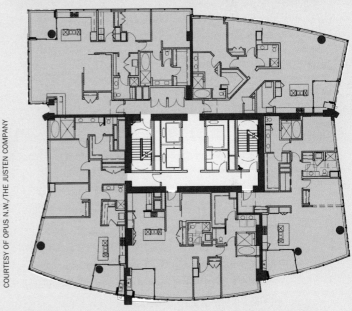

COURTESY OF OPUS N.W./THE JUSTEN COMPANY

Floor plans show five units per floor and three per floor. The small floor plate (about 10,700 square feet) and large units (averaging 1,900 square feet) reflect a new trend in residential towers.

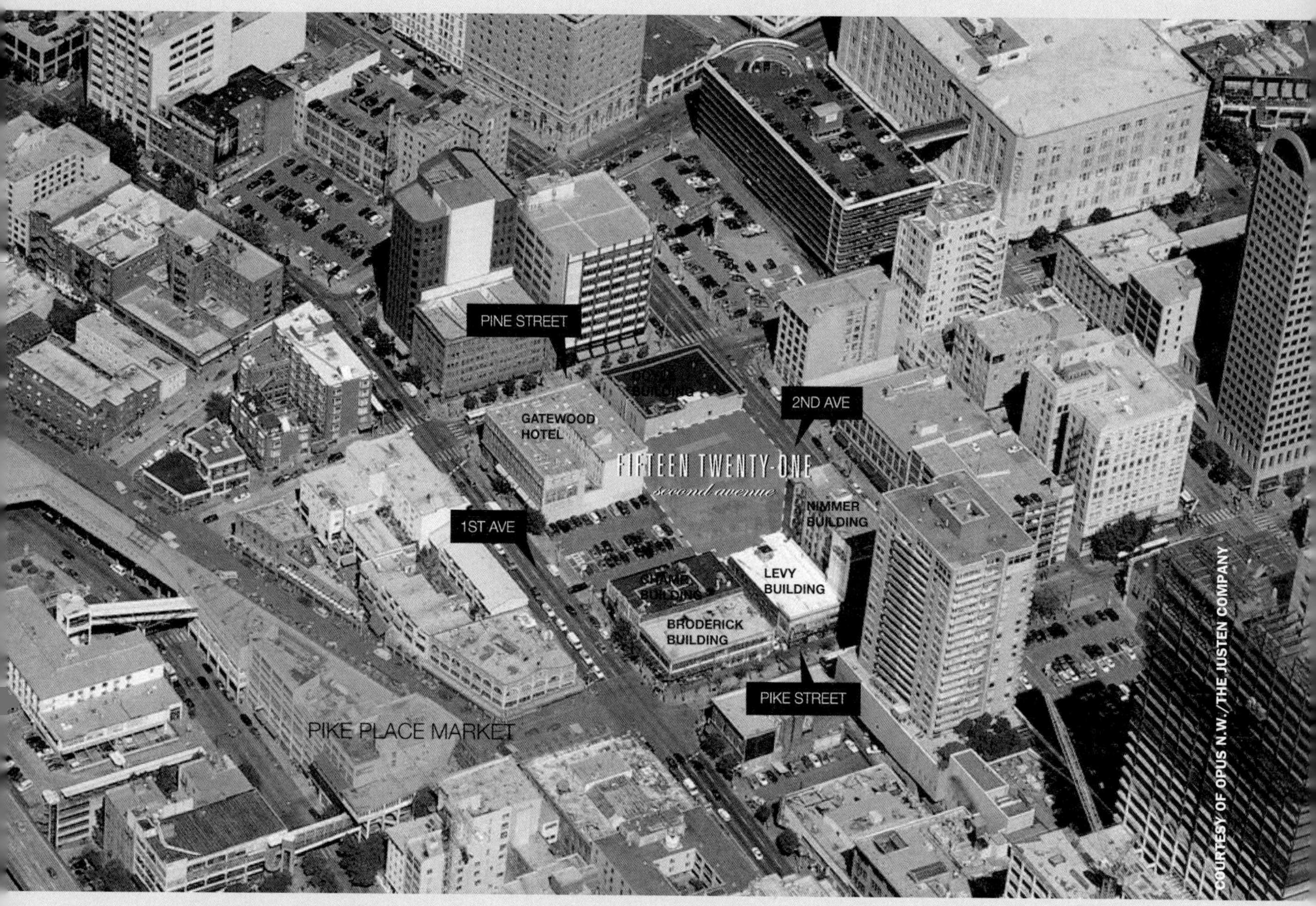
PINE STREET
GATEWOOD HOTEL
2ND AVE
FIFTEEN TWENTY-ONE
second avenue
1ST AVE
NIMMER BUILDING
LEVY BUILDING
BRODERICK BUILDING
PIKE STREET
PIKE PLACE MARKET

COURTESY OF OPUS N.W./THE JUSTEN COMPANY

**Fifteen Twenty-One Second Avenue will stand a half block from Pike Street Market on a redeveloping block.**

Dexter Apartments on South Lake Union, 180 condominiums at Harbor Square on Bainbridge Island, and the recently completed, 220-unit, M-Street apartments at 8th and Madison. Justen's downtown residential portfolio includes condominiums at the top of Market Place Tower at First and Lenora and in the Pike and Virginia Building, both near Fifteen Twenty-One Second Avenue, and two loft projects in Pioneer Square. His condominium living and downtown development of Market Place North, the Pike and Virginia Building, and others brought extensive firsthand experience of how condominium owners want to live in their homes and the city.

Design architect Weber + Thompson's slender residential tower reflects trends in nearby Vancouver, British Columbia, and elsewhere on the West Coast. Units at Fifteen Twenty-One Second Avenue are between 1,600 and 2,700 square feet

(149 and 251 square meters) in size. There are five units on each of floors 7 through 29, four each on 30 through 35, and only three units per floor on 36, 37, and 38. Plans are irregular in shape, and the sweeping, floor-to-ceiling water and city views dominate open living areas.

Instead of a traditional balcony, each unit has a feature Justen calls a "glass room," a large, glass-enclosed solarium with a stone-slab fireplace. The accordion-fold upper half of the outer glass wall of each solarium can be fully opened in good weather, and the half-wall below serves as a glass guardrail. Finishes and fixtures are penthouse quality throughout the tower. A landscaped rooftop terrace has a kitchen for grilling and a fireplace. Hotel-type extras include conference space, a fitness center, and concierge service.

A midblock connector concourse provides covered vehicular access for drop-off and pick-up, direct access to Second Avenue, and pedestrian circulation from Second Avenue. The 20-foot-high (6.1-meter-high) lobby is conceived as a meeting area for residents, with seating near a large basalt stone fireplace. During the design review process, the developer was granted a departure allowing for a slight reduction in the required storefront retail in return for these street-activating features.

Perhaps the most unusual element of the project is the outer layer of work/studio spaces in the base. Each about the size of a double parking stall in plan, 28 workspace/studios extend four levels above the street-level storefronts. These activate the street corridor and buffer the parking from view, as required in the new code. Avid buyers, all tower condominium owners, plan to use them for a variety of purposes, including art studio, wine cellar, and sound studio, as well as office.

The project is expected to qualify for LEED Silver certification based on a number of factors that include energy- and water-saving fixtures, locally sourced materials, mechanical systems, and proximity to mass transit. LEED certification is required to be able to add floor area through the housing bonus program.

Originally caught up in plans for a monorail station in the base, the project underwent an interactive permitting process that not only determined many aspects of the building design but also helped shape certain features of the new downtown zoning code. Well aware of the mayor and city council's intention to make changes to the code, Opus and Justen made a permit application for the 400-foot (121.92-meter) condominium tower through a legal provision called a text amendment, in which the developer assumed risk for building above the height limit, then 240 feet (73.15 meters). The code was changed and the permit issued just prior to the start of construction based on the new code.

In a market where typical condominium towers have units priced anywhere from $200,000 (studios) to over $2 million (penthouses), presale prices at Fifteen Twenty-One Second Avenue started at $750,000. Prospective buyers visit a model unit, tucked into a nearby downtown building. Of 143 units, nine remained unsold as of August 2007.

# University Neighborhood Overlay, Austin, Texas

The Austin City Council enacted the University Neighborhood Overlay (UNO) district on September 2, 2004. An incentive-based zoning overlay that allows greater densities and encourages affordable housing while providing design guidelines for an improved streetscape and pedestrian experience, the district encompasses the West Campus neighborhood near the University of Texas (UT). It also consolidates student housing near campus, relieving pressure to redevelop single-family homes in nearby neighborhoods.

The UNO is an example of the city, private sector, and concerned neighbors working together. A major reason for its success is that a coalition of neighborhoods brought a workable solution of design standards to the city, which, following numerous public meetings to work out details, folded those standards into a zoning overlay that the city council unanimously approved.

*Contact information:*

Mark Walters
Principal Planner, Neighborhood Planning and
    Zoning Department
City of Austin
505 Barton Springs Road, 5th Floor
Austin, TX 78704
512-974-7668

*www.ci.austin.tx.us*

## Community Information

The city of Austin, Texas, has an estimated 2007 population of 735,000 in a metropolitan area of just over 1.5 million, according to the U.S. Census Bureau. The metropolitan area has been growing at a rate of 2 to 4 percent per year since 2000. Major employers include the University of Texas (20,200 employees), Dell (16,400), the city of Austin (11,800), Austin Independent School District (10,400), and Freescale Semiconductor, Inc. (8,100).

Austin has a city manager form of government. Six council members and a mayor may serve two three-year terms. An official coalition of neighborhood groups was formed to advise the UNO process.

The West Campus neighborhood had a population of 12,500 as of the 2000 census, although because of the high student population, that number fluctuates greatly during the year and is more difficult to estimate as a result. Nonetheless, since 2000, substantial development has taken place, largely because of the UNO, so the population of the neighborhood may reach as much as 20,000 by 2010.

Guadalupe Street forms the eastern border of the neighborhood. It is nearly one mile (1.61 km) north-south and slightly less east-west. Lined with mostly retail uses along its western side, Guadalupe Street divides the UT campus from the residential neighborhood to the west. Generally, land use in the West Campus neighborhood becomes less intense from east to west, traveling farther from campus. Correspondingly, students live in greater densities in the east of the neighborhood, where more apartment properties are available, and less so to the northwest and southwest, where single-family homes are more common. Still, the entire neighborhood is decidedly a mix of rental and owner-occupied housing.

Guadalupe Street is the primary north-south road serving the neighborhood. Several other north-south streets, some of which are one way, handle a large amount of local traffic. East-west streets handle additional automobile traffic as well, but they are also key pedestrian corridors that provide routes to and from the UT campus.

## Impetus and Early Planning

The University of Texas has about 50,000 students, but only 7,000 of them live on campus in official university housing. Thus, considerable demand exists for housing close to campus. This market creates a significant opportunity for developers that can find available sites but at the same time is a source of concern for many residents in surrounding neighborhoods who do not want to deal with the noise, crowding, and parking problems associated with the student population.

In 2002, a 150-unit, four-story apartment development called the Villas of Guadalupe opened along Guadalupe Street, just north of campus and immediately south of a historic and stable single-family neighborhood. Nearby residents opposed the project, and although it went ahead, neighborhood groups continued to object.

The city of Austin did not want a protracted fight against student housing development every time a project was proposed, so it began a planning process with neighborhoods surrounding the UT campus. Six neighborhood groups created the Central Austin Neighborhood Planning Advisory Committee (CANPAC) to formally work with the city on the issue.

Compounding the problem was a loophole in the city code that allowed a single-family lot to be developed with duplexes that contained six bedrooms on each side. The result was what the city and residents call "super-duplexes" of up to 40 feet (12.19 meters) in height, housing 12 or more residents. The planning process for the UNO closed this loophole.

The ultimate solution created by the neighborhood planning process resulted in the University Neighborhood Overlay. The neighborhood planning process included land use regulations to protect the character of the surrounding historic neighborhoods. University Area Partners, one of the six neighborhood groups that make up CANPAC, hired an architect to create design standards, most of which were folded into the approved version of the UNO.

The planning process was by no means easy. From the first official public meeting to final approval of the UNO took nearly two years, involving a wide range of stakeholders from concerned neighbors to affected property owners. The first public meeting for the UNO process was held in December 2002, and the UNO was passed unanimously in September 2004.

PHOTO BY SAM NEWBERG

**The University Neighborhood Overlay provides density incentives in exchange for affordable housing allowances and streetscape improvements.**

## Details

The UNO is a subset of the existing zoning code for the area and essentially overrides it. The primary differences are (a) it allows much greater density, primarily through increased building height, and (b) it requires the developer to create a high-quality streetscape and provide for affordable housing.

A core area of the West Campus area nearest the UT campus allows a maximum height of 175 feet (53.34 meters). The maximum allowed height tapers down farther away from campus and is 40 to 60 feet (12.19 to 18.29 meters) at the edge of the neighborhood. Exceptions of 15 feet (4.57 meters) of additional height are allowed if additional affordable housing is provided.

For the most part, the UNO does not have minimum setbacks. Instead, most properties have maximum setbacks of 10 feet (3.05 meters). This strategy encourages a dense urban environment, with most buildings built up to or near the public sidewalk.

The transportation system through the neighborhood is complex. Guadalupe Street is a major two-way street separating the UT campus and the West Campus neighborhood. It is the primary north-south street in the area, although several other one-way streets provide good vehicular access through West Campus. East-west streets in the West Campus neighborhood are generally narrower and focused on pedestrian and bicycle traffic to and from campus. Streetscape improvements as part of the UNO will further widen sidewalks and improve pedestrian circulation. Transit serves the area reasonably well, including several express bus routes specifically for UT students. Still, city staff members observe that a major percentage of students own and use cars for a significant proportion of trips.

For housing developments in the UNO, developers are required to set aside 10 percent of all units to households earning 80 percent or less of the area median income (AMI). In addition, developers have the option of (a) making 10 percent of units available to households earning 65 percent of AMI or (b) paying 50 cents per square foot of net rentable floor area to an affordable housing fund specifically directed to housing in the neighborhood. The AMI for Austin in March 2006 was $45,500 for a family of two.

To avoid excessive height on the portion of buildings that face streets, the UNO requires setbacks or step-backs. Buildings over 60 feet (18.29 meters) in height must have facades that step back 12 feet (3.66 meters). Furthermore, buildings over 60 feet (18.29 meters) high must be stepped back farther

More than 2,300 new residential units have been developed since the 2004 approval of the UNO.

from the north edge of the site, according to a formula to reduce shadows on adjacent properties.

Nearly half of all building area facing a street must contain occupied space, either commercial or residential, and cannot be parking or mechanical. This requirement still allows pedestrian and garage doors, but it avoids blank walls facing streets, thus enhancing the pedestrian environment.

Developers are required to construct sidewalks no less than 12 feet (3.66 meters) wide and must plant trees and install "pedestrian-scale" streetlighting, according to city standards. Intended to foster a very dense urban fabric, the UNO does not have any particular open-space requirements. Streetscape enhancements in the public rights-of-way are considered sufficient. An extensive park and open-space system consisting of Pease Park and the Shoal Creek Hike and Bike Trail is located immediately west of the West Campus neighborhood.

Parking is handled in a number of ways. Construction of new surface parking for commercial uses is prohibited. For new developments, parking must be on street, underground, or in ramps. A 40 percent parking reduction is allowed for residential uses that participate in a car-sharing program. Commercial uses of less than 20,000 square feet (1,858 square meters) along commercial corridors are not required to provide off-street parking.

The effect of the UNO has been significant. Since approval and implementation of the UNO, a substantial amount of new development has occurred in the West Campus neighborhood, much of it housing targeted to students. As of October 2006, two years after passage of the UNO, approximately 2,360 units in the West Campus area had been built, were under construction, or had entered the development review process. The city expects 7,000 to 10,000 units to be built as a result of the UNO.

Community-driven design guidelines promote tree-lined streetscapes and an improved pedestrian experience.

PHOTO BY SAM NEWBERG

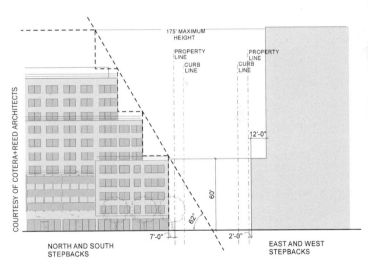

COURTESY OF COTERA+REED ARCHITECTS

The overlay district mandates building step-backs for new development, ensuring a human scale for the neighborhood.

The Texan, one of the first projects developed under the UNO, was originally submitted to the city as a 23-unit concept. Within days of the UNO approval, the developer resubmitted the plan with 62 units to take advantage of the increased density permitted on the site. Any developer that chooses to participate in the UNO can take advantage of a substantial increase in the number of units allowed.

A visual comparison of pre- and post-UNO development is striking in terms of quantity and quality. The design-related elements of the UNO ensure a pedestrian-friendly environment. Whereas previous development may have a variety of elements, such as blank ground-floor exterior walls, paved areas in front of buildings used for parking, or a lack of streetscaping, the UNO addresses all of these elements and more. Even with much greater density, all new development has occupied residential or commercial first-floor space and streetscap-

ing with wide sidewalks and tree plantings. Even parking garages have first-floor retail space.

One developer noted that most of the larger sites have been developed or redeveloped. Many remaining sites are single-family homes, which are typically small and more difficult to assemble than single, larger sites. This situation will likely slow future development, as developers are forced to wait until appropriately sized sites can be assembled before development commences.

## Lessons Learned

Strong leadership was the most important factor in getting the UNO approved. It is important not only that elected officials support the policy of increased density, but that the neighborhood groups do, as well, and that the two enjoy a healthy relationship.

Perhaps the most important key to success of the UNO is that it is an incentive-based system rather than being restrictive. Clearly, the density allowed under the UNO is an incentive to developers, because they can develop up to three times the number of units allowed under the underlying zoning.

Nearly everyone is surprised by the rate at which development has taken place. With approximately 2,300 units built or approved, pent-up demand for student housing clearly existed. The pace of development is placing a strain on utilities in the neighborhood. In retrospect, the city departments responsible for utility maintenance and upgrades should have been involved in the UNO process earlier and been better prepared for a rapid development rate.

PHOTO BY SAM NEWBERG

The UNO allows up to three times the density permitted by the underlying zoning and is spurring residential development throughout the West Campus neighborhood.

## Featured Development: Quarters on Campus

The Quarters on Campus is a series of developments by Simmons Vedder & Co. in various locations throughout the West Campus neighborhood. Already open and occupied are three buildings in Phase I, consisting of the Quarters at Cameron House, with 64 units; Montgomery House, with 88 units; and Sterling House, with 100 units.

Building design is typically five stories, with ground-floor retail and enclosed parking, and four stories of residential units above. Construction materials consist of a ground-floor concrete "podium" and wood framing on the upper floors. The three buildings contain between 1,300 and 5,600 square feet (121 and 520 meters) of ground-floor retail space.

With 252 units in Phase I, the Cameron, Montgomery, and Sterling Houses share six floor plans with two types of one-, two-, and three-bedroom units. Floor plans feature a common area with kitchen and living space, and a separate private bathroom for every bedroom. Overall, there are 480 bedrooms, some of which allow double occupancy. The developers estimate that if occupancy were maximized, Phase I would have 704 residents.

The three Phase I buildings contain 427 parking stalls, excluding on-street parking. That equates to a parking ratio of 1.7 stalls per unit or 0.9 stall per bedroom, which assumes that nearly every resident has a car, except roommate situations.

Phase II will include the Quarters at Nueces House, with 235 units; the Quarters at Grayson House, with 101 units; and the Quarters Garage, with 12 units, 49,000 square feet (4,552 square meters) of retail space, and 225 garage stalls. A third phase, called the Quarters at Bandera House, will have 250 more apartment units. All three phases will total 850 units, about 10 percent of all units forecast to be developed in the West Campus neighborhood.

The Phase I unit mix is generally divided equally between one-, two-, and three-bedroom layouts. Reflecting perceived unit demand, Phase II will add a number of efficiencies and a few four-bedroom units, although overall, two-bedroom floor plans will represent nearly one-half of the unit mix.

PHOTO BY SAM NEWBERG

Phase I of The Quarters on Campus consists of 252 residential units atop ground-floor retail and enclosed parking.

# City of Villages, San Diego, California

With the intention of encouraging mixed-use villages close to transit that feature housing, retail, jobs, and civic uses in pedestrian-friendly environments, the city of San Diego adopted the City of Villages (COV) growth strategy in 2002 when it adopted the "Strategic Framework"—the first element of the city's 2002 update to its General Plan. The impetus for the COV strategy began in 1999, when the city of San Diego embarked upon the first update to its General Plan in 20 years. The city selected five "pilot villages" to begin implementing the COV strategy in 2004.

*Contact information:*
William Anderson
Director
City Planning & Community Investment
City of San Diego, 202 C Street, MS 5A
San Diego, CA 92101
Phone: 619-235-5200
E-mail: andersonw@sandiego.gov

*Web site:*
www.sandiego.gov/planning/

## City of San Diego Community Information

The city of San Diego covers 330 square miles (854.7 square km) and has a population of more than 1.3 million residents. The major industries in San Diego include manufacturing, defense, and tourism. However, the San Diego economy has diversified in the last decade to include telecommunications, software, and biotechnology, which are among San Diego's fastest-growing industries. These "brain power" industries benefit from San Diego's excellent higher-education facilities, including the University of California, San Diego, which is world renowned for its science programs.

COURTESY OF CITY OF SAN DIEGO

An integral part of San Diego's 2002 General Plan update, the City of Villages development strategy is designed to encourage mixed-use villages across a diverse collection of neighborhoods.

San Diego is the seventh-largest city in the United States and the second largest in California. The population of San Diego increased sharply from 875,000 in 1980 to 1,305,000 in 2005, representing a nearly 50 percent increase. The population over the next 25 years is forecast to continue to increase, albeit at a slower pace, to 1,656,000 in 2030 (or by 27 percent).

San Diego's diverse array of housing types includes apartments, downtown condominiums, suburban single-family homes, and luxury oceanfront or canyon estates. According to the U.S. Census, 49 percent of the housing units in the city are owner occupied. The majority of the housing stock (or 59 percent) has been built since 1970.

## About the City of Villages Growth Strategy

The San Diego City Council approved the five "pilot village" demonstration projects in February 2004. The five villages are dispersed throughout the city and represent a variety of approaches to revitalizing existing neighborhoods. The project teams are diverse and include local neighborhood community groups, partnerships between developers and community groups, and a public university. Table 8 summarizes key characteristics of each pilot village plan.

**The Boulevard Marketplace** pilot village is located in Mid-City within the Normal Heights planning area along El Cajon Boulevard adjacent to the Route 15 Freeway. The surrounding area has one of the highest residential densities in San Diego. In addition, the major transportation artery (Interstate 15) bisects what was once a cohesive neighborhood. The Boulevard Marketplace consists of two phases on 16 acres (6.47 hectares) of land. Phase I calls for 366 housing units, including row homes, condominiums, and apartments (including 20 percent affordable units) as well 40,000 square feet (3,716 square meters) of retail space and another 40,000 square feet (3,716 square meters) of office uses.

**Mi Pueblo** pilot village is located in the southern edge of the city immediately north of the U.S.-Mexican border. Mi Pueblo covers 22 acres (8.9 hectares) located along the historic commercial core of San Ysidro Boulevard. The goal is to revitalize an aging, underused commercial district while enhancing the pedestrian orientation of the community. The plan envisions more than 1,100 new residential units (including 25 percent affordable housing), as well as commercial uses, a civic

plaza, parking structures, possibly a library, and office space for community-serving groups.

**Village Center at Euclid and Market** is located at the intersection of four neighborhoods in the southeastern area of San Diego: Chollas View, Lincoln Park, Emerald Hills, and Valencia Park. The village covers 45 acres (18.21 hectares), and the plan calls for residential, commercial, and civic uses. The site plan for the Village Center takes advantage of the area's topography with terraced residential units enjoying views of Chollas Creek and beyond. The site plan focuses on improving Chollas Creek as a waterway and linear park for the community. Upon completion, the village will include 839 new residential units (with a majority affordable to low- and moderate-income households), retail and office space, and civic uses.

**North Park Village** is located 3 miles (4.83 km) northeast of downtown San Diego, immediately north of Balboa Park. The formerly neglected area was already experiencing a renaissance at the time of the pilot village designation. The plan for the North Park pilot village is a combination of several catalyst projects spread out over 40 acres (16.19 hectares), including new multifamily housing, streetscape improvements, storefront renovation, new civic

---

**Table 8: FIVE PILOT VILLAGES**

| Pilot Village | Acres | Proposed Housing Units | Density (Dwelling Units/Acre) | Proposed Commercial (Square Feet) | Redevelopment Area | Business Improvement District |
|---|---|---|---|---|---|---|
| Boulevard Marketplace | 8 | 366 | 50 | 80,000 | Yes | Yes |
| Mi Pueblo | 22 | 1,143 | 10 to 64 | 150,000 | Yes | Yes |
| Village Center | 45 | 839 | 28.3 | To be determined | Yes | Yes |
| North Park | 40 | 483 | 50 to 75 | To be determined | Yes | Yes |
| The Paseo | 11 | 461 | 46 | 364,000 | Yes | Yes |

*Source: City of San Diego.*

COURTESY OF CITY OF SAN DIEGO

Each village is designed to be pedestrian-friendly and connected to the regional transit system.

uses, and a focus on supporting and expanding the community's art and cultural uses. The plan calls for making North Park a prime destination for arts patrons (see "Featured Development").

**The Paseo** is located adjacent to the San Diego State University (SDSU) campus. It is planned as an 11-acre (4.45-hectare) mixed-use urban village where students, faculty, staff, and local residents can live, work, dine, shop, study, and play. The plan calls for retail, offices, cafés, and student housing as well as a multiplex movie theater that will serve as lecture halls for SDSU during weekday mornings. The site plan focuses on an enhanced pedestrian experience and transit access because it is contiguous to the SDSU trolley station and bus transit center (which opened in 2005).

## Community Government and Political Structure

The city of San Diego is governed by a city council consisting of eight members elected by district and a mayor who is elected citywide. The San Diego Planning Commission is a seven-member body appointed to four-year terms by the council. The city's primary planning document is the General Plan, which outlines the citywide land use plans and goals. Because of San Diego's size

and diversity, it has more than 40 planning areas that have their own community plans. These Community Plans are intended to implement the General Plan and are consistent with the policies and recommendations of the General Plan.

The Community Plans address the development of land within specific neighborhoods and provide more-detailed land use, design, and infrastructure information than at the General Plan level. This type of structure recognizes the diversity of each of San Diego's neighborhoods while allowing the General Plan to focus on citywide development issues.

## Policy Analysis

With the adoption of the City of Villages, San Diego aims to target growth in differently scaled urban villages that include a mix of housing, commercial, employment, schools, and civic uses in areas where a high level of activity already exists. The strategy is to build on existing neighborhoods to create lively activity hubs and improve walkability in districts close to transit. The initial goal was to complete construction in three to five years.

As outlined in the Strategic Framework Element, the COV growth strategy provided the "vision" for

COURTESY OF CITY OF SAN DIEGO

**The City of Villages strategy is aimed at bolstering existing neighborhoods by providing a lively mix of retail, housing, and employment opportunities.**

the update to the rest of the city's General Plan. The COV strategy emphasizes the coordination of land use and transit by locating village centers along major transit corridors. The COV plan also calls for increasing housing through infill and redevelopment of aging commercial centers. The plan's emphasis on concentrating housing and employment in transit-served areas has the benefit of improving the jobs/housing balance within communities as well as the city at large. However, the COV plan does not recommend specific density targets or goals for communities. The actual designation of villages and the specific policies and implementation of the COV strategy was deferred to the city's community planning areas. As noted previously, the five pilot villages involved applications by various community groups. As described in the Strategic Framework, the ideal pilot villages are located in highly visible and accessible places and serve as an example that may be replicated in the other neighborhoods.

As Bill Anderson, the director of planning for the city of San Diego, notes, "The pilot villages are focused planning and redevelopment efforts to create examples for what type of development is possible in a variety of densities and scales." The actual land use plan for each pilot village was determined in the community plans for that

particular portion of the city. To encourage development in the pilot villages, the San Diego City Council adopted a series of incentives in 2003 that included the following:

- Granting priority to pilot villages for infrastructure upgrades or replacements;
- Deferring collection of fees;
- Providing funding sources for items such as accessibility, rebates on property taxes, and revolving loan funds; and
- Providing assistance related to policies and regulations on the undergrounding of utilities, affordable housing, and Community Development Block Grants.

## Process of COV Enactment

The city of San Diego last updated its General Plan in 1979, when the city still had large tracts of undeveloped land. By the late 1990s, the city was more than 90 percent built out. However, with a population projected to increase 27 percent by 2030 (to 1.65 million), the growth must be accommodated by infill and redevelopment. As Planning Director Bill Anderson notes, "The City of Villages is aimed at targeting growth in existing areas." Another key concern underlying the COV strategy was that the infrastructure in the city's urban neighborhoods had not kept pace with growth. With that in mind, the COV's incentives were aimed at improving public facilities and infrastructure in concert with the new growth targeted to the pilot villages. Table 9 highlights the key milestones in the development of the COV growth strategy.

The Strategic Framework element was developed through an intensive process of public collaboration over a three-year period. As noted, the Strategic Framework was drafted to serve as the "vision" for the city's update of the General Plan. The planning for the Strategic Framework included the work of several topical committees consisting of key stakeholders, such as residents and labor, environment, business, and city representatives. The topics covered by the committees included community character, economic prosperity, and public facility finance. In addition, numerous public workshops were held across the city.

After the city council adopted the Strategic Framework in 2002, the city began to solicit proposals for pilot villages that would best demonstrate the goals and vision of the COV strategy. Developers and community groups formed teams to submit proposals. Although local community stakeholders devised the proposals, there was some neighborhood opposition caused by perceptions about increased density. However, given the city's budgetary crisis in the early 2000s (largely caused by pension underfunding), at least some of the opposition reflected concerns about a funding shortfall for infrastructure rather than actual opposition to the proposed village plans. At the same time, the involvement of local community

stakeholders as the applicants for the pilot villages encouraged community participation and ultimately acceptance of the plans.

The city selected five pilot villages that are dispersed throughout the city and represent a variety of approaches. One common trait of each of the winning proposals was that each applicant had pulled together a complete proposal with a vision for implementation in a three-to-five-year period.

## Effect of the COV

The implementation of the COV pilot villages has not proceeded as quickly as originally envisioned. The reasons include organizational difficulties, multiple property ownerships, the lack of a funding mechanism for infrastructure, and the financial crisis that beset the city in recent years. In addition, as collaborative efforts, the pilot villages involve multiple stakeholders (for example, community groups, residents, and business owners) and property owners. Even with broad consensus for the pilot village plans, such collaborative efforts often take longer than anticipated.

### Table 9: MILESTONES IN DEVELOPING COV STRATEGY

| Date | Event |
|---|---|
| 1999 | City begins planning for the Stategic Framework |
| March 2002 | Planning Commission recommends adoption of Strategic Framework |
| October 2002 | City Council adopts Strategic Framework element |
| December 2002 | Pilot Village application/selection process begins |
| October 2003 | Pilot Villages final applications submitted |
| November 2003 | Pilot Village incentives approved |
| January 2004 | Planning Commission recommends five Pilot Village proposals |
| February 2004 | City Council selects Pilot Villages |

Despite the challenges, signs of new development and redevelopment in pilot villages are beginning to emerge. Although the implementation of the pilot villages will take longer than expected, the projects underway are providing concrete examples of how the city's existing neighborhoods can evolve with a greater mix of uses. For example, in North Park, the historic North Park Theatre has been restored, a new parking garage has been completed, and a new mixed-use condominium development is complete (see "Featured Development").

The implementation of the COV has been slower than planned in part because the city was beset with multiple investigations into its pension deficit. With a new mayor and planning director, the pilot villages are getting renewed attention that should help move projects along at a faster pace. The lack of financing for infrastructure improvements in the pilot villages also led to the slower than expected implementation. When the city council approved the plan in 2002, it left the infrastructure issue unaddressed. In the current update to its General Plan, the city is expected to include an infrastructure finance plan.

## Lessons Learned

Engaging the public is important, so they understand that smart growth is not just a strategy to increase density. As Bill Anderson, the director of planning, notes: "Sometimes developers are not adept at addressing how smart growth will improve a community's character. The public needs to see that urban infill improves their quality of life. That is why we need real life examples to demonstrate it." According to Anderson, the city needs five to ten more village designations to

To promote a vibrant mix of uses, the North Park village plan encourages residential development alongside cultural and art establishments.

COURTESY OF DR HORTON

accommodate growth over the next ten to 15 years. Moreover, if implemented as envisioned, the COV strategy will affect only about 5 to 8 percent of San Diego's total land area.

Offering more examples of successful villages not only demonstrates the potential of smart growth, but it also shows that compact development can be expressed in a myriad of ways and that no "one-size-fits-all" solutions exist for smart growth. As General Plan program manager for the city Nancy Brogado states: "With over 40 community planning areas in San Diego, it would be challenging to have a one-size-fits-all approach. For this reason, the COV strategy and our new General Plan are best viewed as a 'toolkit' or a 'menu of options' that communities may use depending on the circumstance."

Finally, development cannot begin without public infrastructure. As Anderson notes, "It is crucial to have a strategy and mechanism in place to fund the public infrastructure required to encourage urban infill."

## Featured Development: North Park

North Park is located approximately three miles (4.83 km) northeast of downtown San Diego and was designated a pilot village in 2004. The neighborhood is bounded by Balboa Park and Switzer Canyon on the south, Florida Street to the west, El Cajon Boulevard on the north, and Interstate 805 to the east. North Park's "downtown" area is centered at the intersection of University Avenue and 30th Street.

The North Park neighborhood first developed as a streetcar suburb in the early part of the 20th century. The neighborhood's housing stock includes Craftsman-style bungalows built in the early 1900s. The North Park commercial district along University Avenue contains a variety of 20th-century architectural styles, including Streamline moderne, art deco, and Mediterranean. From the 1930s to the immediate post–World War II period, North Park was a vibrant commercial district with regional retail stores and small offices. However, by 1960 the economic vitality of the North Park commercial and residential areas was in decline. Beginning in the late 1990s, the area began to turn around, seeing residential redevelopment and an influx of arts and entertainment uses.

The coapplicants to designate North Park a pilot village were North Park Main Street and the North Park Community Association. These two community-based nonprofit organizations viewed San Diego's City of Villages as an opportunity to capitalize on the still nascent renaissance occurring in North Park. The North Park pilot village proposal focused on a variety of catalytic projects in the downtown area rather than concentrating on just one project.

To encourage a lively mix of uses, North Park's pilot village plan reinforces existing commercial and civic uses while promoting new residential, art, and cultural uses to create an active downtown for residents and visitors. The following projects were identified in the North Park pilot village plan as catalytic projects that would further the transformation of downtown North Park. Although many of these projects were already in the works before the pilot village designation, the visibility and attention brought by the COV created additional momentum for them:

The Birch North Park Theatre, a historic live theater in North Park, reopened in 2005 after extensive renovations, serving as a regional entertainment destination.

COURTESY OF CITY OF SAN DIEGO

The North Park parking structure, located across the street from the Birch North Park Theatre, incorporates public art installations and ground-floor retail.

**North Park Theatre Restoration:** The historic North Park Theatre opened its doors for the first time in over 20 years in 2005. The restored former movie palace is now serving as a regional destination for live theater.

**North Park Theatre Parking Structure:** This four-deck parking and retail structure was constructed directly across the street from the North Park Theatre. The facility includes a flexible arts feature that allows original art to be displayed on the facade. The project was funded in partnership with the redevelopment agency and a private developer.

**La Boheme Condominiums:** La Boheme is the largest development project built in North Park in several decades. The mixed-use project by DR Horton includes 224 residential units (including 55 affordable units) and approximately 15,000 square feet (1,394 square meters) of ground-floor retail. The community features a courtyard spa, a social lounge, and a fitness center.

The mixed-use La Boheme contains 224 residential units— 55 of which are affordable—and over 15,000 square feet of ground-floor retail.

**Walgreens and San Diego National Bank Parking Structure:** Located at 32nd Street and University Avenue, this project includes a single-story Walgreens drugstore with adjacent retail space and a two-deck parking structure behind an existing bank.

# Chapter 4

# Tools for Success: Achieving Compact Development and Higher Densities

THE FOLLOWING CHAPTER EXAMINES A COLLECTION of policies, tools, and resources used by localities and organizations across the country to encourage compact development. For each program type, the toolkit includes a brief overview and offers examples. Ranging widely in size and scope, the toolkit is intended to demonstrate the diversity and innovation deployed in pursuit of getting density right.

# Codes

Codes are among the most widely used tools in shaping the built environment and have been around for a long time. Recent innovations have demonstrated that codes can be powerful tools in creating workable density.

## Form-Based Codes

Form-based codes are an alternative to conventional zoning, used to encourage a mix of land uses. This regulatory tool focuses on the physical design of buildings—rather than land uses—as a means of establishing compatibility in neighborhoods. Form-based codes establish rules for building height and bulk, building setbacks, site layout, configuration of public open space, parking location, and streetscape design; they are frequently accompanied by graphics to illustrate permitted development. Although form-based codes establish the physical form and outline of the structures, they tend to allow almost any mixture of uses within the prescribed physical form.

Density regulations under form-based codes often indicate minimum as well as maximum densities. Form-based codes encourage density in appropriate locations, such as transit stops and downtown streets. Although compact development is not automatically a result of form-based codes, the ability to mix uses more readily encourages creating higher-density, walkable, pedestrian-friendly communities. Since form-based codes do not focus on the regulation of uses, the resulting development can better respond to changing markets. Later conversion to other uses may be easier as well, at least from a regulatory perspective. Because the adoption of form-based codes requires significant upfront community involvement, using such codes can reduce community opposition later in the development process.

## Keys to Success

Several conditions must exist for the successful adoption of form-based zoning, including the following:
- A thorough and substantial comprehensive land use plan is the critical foundation for a meaningful form-based code.
- In some states, local governments need a legal go-ahead from state government to make substantial changes in land use law.
- Community understanding and support for a major shift in land development codes, and understanding of the difference between traditional zoning and form-based codes.

Because a complete overhaul of an existing zoning code is clearly a challenge, many communities have sought to find a careful balance between the status quo and innovation. For example, in the Louisville, Kentucky, metropolitan area, planners decided to keep the existing zoning code to address uses and density, but they replaced the design guidelines with form districts that must meet the design requirements for height, design, and orientation, no matter what the use is.

Form-based codes may be especially useful in governing infill development in established neighborhoods with a consistent form that the code can reinforce or replicate.

## Examples and Resources

### Petaluma, California

http://cityofpetaluma.net/cdd/cpsp.html

Central Petaluma, a 400-acre (161.87-hectare) area adjacent to Petaluma, California's historic downtown, is the focus of a redevelopment effort and a new form-based code that replaced the city's zoning for the entire area. The new code supports mixed uses and guides the architectural and urban design for the new development much more effectively than the previous conventional zoning could have done and in a form that is more compatible with the older downtown.

### Fort Worth, Texas

http://www.fortworthgov.org/uploadedFiles/Planning/
Zoning_Review/MU_ZoningGuide2006.pdf

The city of Fort Worth, Texas, has developed form-based land use regulations to support mixed uses, based on the city's Comprehensive Plan, which calls for mixed-use growth centers and designated urban villages characterized by compact, pedestrian-scaled, mixed-use neighborhoods and commercial districts. Because these form-based regulations differ significantly from the city's conventional zoning for other commercial districts, Fort Worth has produced an illustrated guide to provide specific examples to support the emphasis on design considerations.

### Arlington County, Virginia

http://www.arlingtonva.us/Departments/
CPHD/Forums/columbia/CPHDForums
ColumbiaColumbiaPikeInitiativeMain.aspx

In some cases, communities find applying the form-based code to a specific area rather than the whole municipality more feasible. In an effort to encourage economic development and mixed uses in what had grown to be an automobile-congested commercial street, the Washington, D.C., suburb of Arlington County, Virginia, has applied a voluntary form-based code to the Columbia Pike corridor since 2003. The county has implemented an alternative, voluntary form-based code and established incentives to encourage its use, such as expedited review. See case study on page 67 of this text.

### Form-Based Codes: Implementing Smart Growth

http://www.lgc.org/freepub/PDF/Land_Use/fact_sheets/
form_based_codes.pdf

The Local Government Commission has published a guide to adopting form-based codes called *Form-Based Codes: Implementing Smart Growth*. Steps covered by the guide include analyzing existing conditions, conducting community visioning, determining an appropriate spatial basis for regulation, developing urban and architectural standards, and illustrating the code.

### SmartCode

http://www.placemakers.com

SmartCode was developed in 2003 by the new urbanist firms Duany Plater Zyberk and PlaceMakers to offer a unified land development ordinance for planning and urban design that includes zoning, subdivision regulations, urban design, and optional architectural standards in one document. Because of its emphasis on the physical form of building and development, the SmartCode is considered a form-based code. It addresses development for blocks and buildings as well as at neighborhood and regional scales.

## Model Codes

Most municipal zoning codes were originally based on a model code issued in the 1920s by the U.S. Department of Commerce. Fortunately, many updated model codes are available to communities seeking alternatives to their existing zoning laws can often turn to model codes to jump-start local code revisions. The codes can be used for many different purposes, such as offering a greater variety of housing options or promoting compact development. Many model codes are produced by state agencies that can also provide technical assistance to modify the code for local purposes.

### How Do They Work?

Model codes can provide concrete guidance for communities in addressing where and when higher densities are appropriate and in providing for higher density in the regulatory code. The following examples refer to a wide range of model codes that can assist communities with appropriate regulatory revisions and additions to support compact development.

### Examples and Resources

**Georgia Alternatives to Conventional Zoning Project**
http://www.dca.state.ga.us/development/PlanningQualityGrowth/programs/modelcode.asp

The Georgia Department of Community Affairs' Alternatives to Conventional Zoning project seeks to provide Georgia's local governments with a set of tools to address land use and development issues. The code offers a variety of alternative approaches to zoning, as well as traditional tools, and addresses relevant code considerations for urban and rural areas, and small downtowns.

**Maryland Smart Neighborhoods and Infill Development Model Codes**
http://www.mdp.state.md.us/pdf/smartneighborhoods.pdf
http://www.mdp.state.md.us/mgs/infill/InfillFinal_1.pdf

The Maryland Department of Planning has produced two model ordinances tailored to municipalities in that state. The report *Smart Neighborhoods* is a model ordinance crafted as an overlay zone designed to help local governments implement mixed-use and compact design without forgoing conventional zoning. It incorporates flexible use regulations, design guidelines, and a streamlined development review procedure. The other report, *Models and Guidelines for Infill Development*, suggests rural, suburban, and urban strategies for infill development.

**Minnesota Model Zoning Technical Advisory Group**
http://www.mnhousing.gov/idc/groups/secure/documents/admin/mhfa_004353.pdf

To identify ways to simplify mixed-use and compact new development and to reduce the cost of infill and redevelopment, the Minnesota Department of Administration's Construction Codes Advisory Council assembled the Model Zoning Technical Advisory Group, a multidisciplinary group of professionals, to analyze regulatory barriers to compact, mixed-use development and redevelopment and to assess how state and local governments can overcome such obstacles.

**Minnesota Planning Model Ordinances for Sustainable Development**
http://www.gda.state.mn.us/pdf/2000/eqb/ModelOrdWhole.pdf

Minnesota Planning prepared model ordinances on selected topics to help local communities implement concepts of sustainable development. The subjects of the model ordinances include citizen participation, growth management, managing community resources, neighborhood design, infrastructure, resource-efficient buildings, and economic development.

## Oregon Commercial and Mixed-Use Development Code Handbook

http://www.oregon.gov/LCD/docs/publications/commmixedusecode.pdf

Under the Oregon Transportation and Growth Management (TGM) Program, a joint program of the Oregon Department of Transportation and the Oregon Department of Land Conservation and Development, Oregon has produced two publications of interest for code assistance. The *Commercial and Mixed-Use Development Code Handbook* shares strategies, best practices, and model ordinances for implementing smart development in commercial and mixed-use areas.

## Oregon Infill and Redevelopment Code Handbook

http://www.oregon.gov/LCD/docs/publications/infilldevcode.pdf

Oregon's *Infill and Redevelopment Code Handbook* provides communities with tools to encourage infill and redevelopment in urban areas by identifying and removing barriers. The report addresses the benefits and barriers to infill and redevelopment, a process for reviewing local conditions, and sample code language to remove regulatory barriers to infill.

## Oregon Small Cities Model Code

http://www.oregon.gov/LCD/TGM/docs/modelCode05/pdf/guide.pdf

Oregon's *Model Development Code and User's Guide for Small Cities* was developed by the state TGM Program in response to many requests for assistance from smaller Oregon communities seeking guidance and technical expertise in zoning, development standards, review procedures, and implementation of state planning rules and statutes. The TGM Program's mission is to maintain and enhance community livability by encouraging compact, pedestrian-friendly development. It also seeks to broaden transportation options and improve development patterns through the integration of land use and transportation planning. The TGM Program provides code assistance services to communities seeking to modify their development, planning, and development review rules to encourage smart growth. The Oregon Department of Transportation and the Oregon Department of Land Conservation and Development jointly sponsor the program.

## American Planning Association

http://www.planning.org/thecommissioner/19952003/summer03.htm

The American Planning Association has many materials to assist local leaders revising local codes. The group has published an article, "Unraveling the Mysteries of Code Writing," that outlines a five-step process for code revision. The article is intended for communities seeking to embark upon code writing and to help them establish consistency between land use plans and regulations.

## American Planning Association Model Smart Land Development Regulations
http://www.planning.org/smartgrowthcodes/

As part of its research on smart land development, the American Planning Association has produced 11 model smart growth codes to help towns, cities, and counties support mixed uses; provide a choice of housing types and transportation modes, including affordable housing; preserve open space and environmentally sensitive areas; and foster a more predictable process for development review.

## LEED for Neighborhood Development
http://www.usgbc.org/DisplayPage.aspx?CMSPageID=148

Designed to integrate the principles of smart growth, urbanism, and green building, the LEED for Neighborhood Development (LEED ND) rating system creates the first national standard for neighborhood design. LEED certification provides independent, third-party verification that a development's location and design meet accepted high standards for environmentally responsible, sustainable, development. LEED ND is a collaboration of the U.S. Green Building Council, the Congress for the New Urbanism, and the Natural Resources Defense Council.

## Local Government Commission Smart Growth Zoning Codes
http://www.lgc.org/freepub/PDF/Land_Use/sg_code_exec_summary.pdf

The Local Government Commission's *Smart Growth Zoning Codes: A Resource Guide* provides examples of 150 smart growth land development codes from around the country that support traditional neighborhood development, mixed uses, transit-oriented development, and context-sensitive street and parking design.

# Renovation Building Codes

Underused older buildings are often ripe for renovation and reuse. Many cities and towns have successfully refurbished old buildings, revitalizing declining neighborhoods and accommodating population growth by using existing infrastructure.

Renovation projects face particular challenges, however. Land assembly and construction can be more costly than greenfield development, and the projects can face a host of regulatory constraints. In recent years, building codes have been created specifically to reflect the realities of rehabilitating existing buildings. This innovation greatly benefits compact development by allowing for the cost-effective reuse of these structures.

Existing buildings in urban centers are often ripe for rehabilitation, and they represent a rich source for new compact development. Often still an essential part of the streetscape's architectural fabric, existing buildings have the advantage of retaining community character if rehabilitated. In some communities, old buildings are subject to additional regulations under historic preservation laws. Conversion of obsolete industrial or commercial buildings to residential uses is often an excellent option for reuse of the building. In other circumstances, existing residential structures would benefit from renovation for revived use.

## Challenges to Building Rehabilitation

Developing building codes that recognize the need for different standards in new construction and the rehabilitation of existing buildings is essential. Traditionally, the building codes that have been designed to ensure the public health and safety of new construction have also governed the rehabilitation of existing buildings. Unfortunately, this uniform approach has frequently required developers to retrofit older structures to modern building standards, making them very costly and difficult to rehabilitate. In particular, the "25–50 percent rule" used by some building codes is problematic. This formula requires rehabilitation projects that cost 50 percent or more of a building's value to bring the entire building into compliance with new construction standards. Projects with renovation costs that come to 25 to 50 percent of the property value have to bring the rehabilitated parts of the building up to code for new construction. Requirements are less stringent for projects that cost less than 25 percent of the building's value. This system frequently discouraged the rehabilitation of otherwise worthy buildings, because property owners had to factor in potentially inflated project costs and technical complications brought on by these requirements. Additionally, many building codes typically required existing buildings to meet a new-construction standard when a change in use occurred, such as converting a former industrial property to residential.

In the last decade, however, led by the U.S. Department of Housing and Urban Development (HUD), with several states following suit, regulators have recognized these challenges to building rehabilitation, as well as the need to be able to reuse existing buildings productively. As a result, several states now have adopted building codes specifically designed for rehabilitation of existing structures, streamlining their redevelopment and fostering the renewal of neighborhoods and communities.

## Examples and Resources

### Maryland Building Rehabilitation Code Program
http://www.mdp.state.md.us

In 2001, the state of Maryland adopted a new, voluntary building rehabilitation code to encourage the renovation of existing buildings. Maryland looked to HUD's *Nationally Applicable Recommended Rehabilitation Provisions (NARRP)* and the New Jersey subcode as models, separating rehabilitation requirements from those for new construction and seeking to make renovations faster and less costly. Counties and municipalities could choose to adopt and amend the code. More recently, Maryland has adopted the 2006 International Existing Building Code (IEBC) as the Maryland Building Rehabilitation Code to take effect in early 2008. The IEBC is a model code produced by the International Code Council, which urges the use of a single set of codes nationwide to bring the entire design and construction industry under the same standards.

### The New Jersey Rehabilitation Subcode
http://www.state.nj.us/dca/codes/rehab

New Jersey adopted a more-flexible, user-friendly rehabilitation subcode for old buildings in 1998. Under this code, renovations to existing buildings are not automatically required to meet all standards for new construction. The subcode contains all the technical requirements that are pertinent to rehabilitation. The state has found that the more-responsive standards of the subcode have reduced by 25 percent the cost of many rehabilitation projects. The code was developed by the New Jersey State Rehabilitation Department of Community Affairs, in coordination with the Rutgers University Center for Urban Policy Research and a steering committee consisting of code officials, fire officials, architects, historic preservationists, advocates for people with disabilities, and government representatives.

### Nationally Applicable Recommended Rehabilitation Provisions

http://www.huduser.org/publications/destech/narrp/toc_narrp.html

Sponsored by the U.S. Department of Housing and Urban Development in 1997, the NARRP was developed and produced in an effort to guide the process of regulating work in existing buildings. The provisions are written to cover the entire range of possible work, from repairs to reconstruction, in all types of structures, including historic buildings. The NARRP is intended for use with minimal adaptation by state and local governments.

### National Trust for Historic Preservation Smart Codes Survey

http://www.nationaltrust.org/smartgrowth/toolkit_codes.pdf

In an effort to offer a survey of practices from around the country, in 2001, the National Trust for Historic Preservation produced "Smart Codes: Smart Growth Tools for Main Street," an issue paper providing an overview of rehabilitation codes adopted by different states and municipalities. The report contains summaries of rehabilitation codes, including New Jersey's and Maryland's statewide codes, California's State Historical Building Code, Chapter 34 of the Massachusetts State Building Code, and a code used in Wichita, Kansas. The publication also cites Wisconsin's 1999 *Smart Growth for Wisconsin* legislation, which requires all cities and villages above 12,500 in population to adopt a model "traditional neighborhood development (TND) ordinance" to encourage pedestrian-friendly and mixed-use developments. (See "Traditional Neighborhood Development" later in this chapter for more information about the Wisconsin law.)

# Zoning

Since the U.S. Supreme Court legitimized land use zoning in the 1926 case *Euclid v. Ambler Realty Co.*, zoning has been one of the core tasks of planners. The concept of separating uses and determining which uses belong in what zones of a city has shaped the development of every American city in the 20th century. Zoning meant people no longer had to live near noxious uses such as factories, and it fostered the creation of large, clean, and safe residential communities. However, the postindustrial economy of the late 20th century and early 21st century changed the equation. With fewer factories and a workforce composed predominantly of knowledge and service workers, the benefits of allowing people to live, work, and shop in the same zones now greatly outweighs the potential risks. Some of the most important innovations in zoning codes that address the changing needs and demands of cities are mixed-use zoning districts, planned unit developments, and overlay zones.

## Mixed-Use Zoning

Mixed-use, compact development typically blends commercial, retail, residential, and civic uses. It allows residents to live closer to where they work and brings shopping nearby, reducing the need for car travel. Appropriately designed mixed uses encourage alternative modes of transportation, including walking, bicycling, and using mass transit. Designating mixed-use zoning districts allows communities to replace traditional zoning that separates land uses. Mixed-use zoning districts are typically stand-alone districts that focus on urban centers and impose specific requirements on the range of permitted uses, development standards, and design criteria.

To encourage the population density needed to sustain nearby commercial uses and to create land use efficiencies, mixed-use districts typically accommodate higher-density residential development. These zoning districts often support construction that includes ground-floor commercial and multifamily residential above, permit higher-density apartment and condominium buildings, or do both.

## Keys to Success

Nearby transit and other transportation options reduce the demand for residential parking spaces and encourage a lively urban environment. Because mixed-use zoning districts are often designated in existing neighborhoods, the zoning specifications should consider existing uses as well as guide future development. Mixed-use compact development is often higher density than the densities in the surrounding community. Although this density is expected and encouraged to better use the limited remaining land in urban areas, successfully integrating the higher-density development with surrounding lower-density residential communities can create a design challenge.

The most important factors in a successful mixed-use zoning district include the following:
- Access to multiple modes of transportation;
- A cohesive and complementary combination of commercial and residential uses;
- A mix of housing types with higher densities;
- Adherence to compatible design standards;
- A pedestrian-friendly orientation; and
- Opportunities for shared or reduced parking.

## Examples

### Plantation, Florida, Midtown District
http://www.plantation.org/pzed/midtown/index.html

The city of Plantation, Florida, sought to transform a suburban, predominantly commercial district into a more-urban, mixed-use town center with the help of a new master plan and zoning district. The new Plantation Midtown Code is designed to guide the appropriate integration of a mix of land uses. It has guided the transformation of the neighborhood from a suburban development pattern to a denser and more active mixed-use town center. See case study on page 47 of this text.

### Albany, Oregon, Mixed-Use Zoning Districts
http://www.ci.albany.or.us/comdev/devcode/pdf/Article_5.pdf

Because they are tailored to individual settings, mixed-use districts can vary widely within a community. The city of Albany, Oregon, is a river town with a population of 44,030, located in the heart of western Oregon's Willamette River valley. Albany has established nine different mixed-use zoning districts to implement the mixed-use concepts envisioned in local comprehensive plans and to distinguish the specific characteristics of different neighborhoods. They include a historic downtown district and downtown central business district that encourage high-density residential infill development.

# Planned Unit Development

Planned unit development (PUD) is a common design and regulatory tool that rural, suburban, and urban communities use to allow more-flexible development of large lots—ranging from a few acres to several hundred—than would be permitted by the underlying zoning. For example, in an area where conventional zoning would simply permit large-lot residential subdivisions, PUDs, as special districts, could allow a mix of housing types and other land uses, such as commercial and open space. PUDs can be designated in advance by the comprehensive plan or be available upon application from the landowner/developer.

## How Do PUDs Support Compact Development?

Local governments can draft a PUD ordinance to permit higher densities, a wider variety of housing types, and more design options than would otherwise be allowed by the underlying zoning district. An area that is zoned for single-family housing can be modified with a residential PUD to allow a variety of housing types, with provisions for appropriate infrastructure. A PUD can be applied to foster a mixed-use development in an area zoned for single use. For example, a community could use a PUD to add residential uses and design review to an area zoned for commercial development. Local government can assign PUDs to designated areas or develop a review process whereby developers can apply for a PUD designation.

One distinction in the development of PUDs, compared to a mixed-use zoning district, is that a PUD is produced by a single developer—a circumstance that can produce economies of scale in the development of the entire site and thus potentially facilitate the production of higher-density housing.

To be most effective, a PUD ordinance should implement goals and objectives included in the community's local comprehensive plan. A community must adopt the PUD as part of its local zoning law, taking care to include clear direction for designating sites for PUD development as well as establishing a process by which the local government will approve applications.

### Examples and Resources

#### Highlands' Garden Village in Denver, Colorado
http://www.highlandsgardenvillage.net/

Formerly the site of an amusement park about three miles (4.83 km) northwest of downtown Denver, Highlands' Garden Village is a thriving, compact, mixed-use redevelopment of 27 acres (10.93 hectares). In 1998, after a two-year public review process, the city of Denver approved the rezoning of the site to be a planned unit development, which allowed more-flexible land development than was otherwise possible under city district zoning regulations. The building designs have emerged from a community-based design review process. The project features narrow streets and a mix of housing types, including owner-occupied single-family homes, townhouses, and both affordable and market-rate rental apartments.

#### New York Guide to Planned Unit Development
http://www.dos.state.ny.us/lgss/pdfs/PUD1.pdf

To assist localities with more-complex zoning techniques, the New York State Legislative Commission on Rural Resources has developed *A Guide to Planned Unit Development*. It covers how local governments can use a PUD to establish more flexibility in their zoning to achieve desired types of development. In addition to PUDs, the publication demonstrates how other codes, such as incentive zoning and cluster development, can effectively preserve community character and open space.

## Overlay Zones

Overlay zones are a method of superimposing additional or alternative regulations over traditional zoning districts. The concept of superimposing the additional or alternative zoning over existing traditional zoning districts makes overlay zones different from some of the tools mentioned previously, many of which replace the underlying zoning. An overlay zone can support additional standards to protect particular natural or cultural features, foster mixed-use development, address specific design concerns, or allow higher-density housing than the surrounding zoning allows. They can be an effective tool for encouraging new development types while, importantly, continuing to allow existing uses. Overlay districts may also be used as alternative stand-alone regulations for managing development.

### How Do They Work?

Communities often adopt mixed-use overlay zones to establish a template for higher-density, mixed-use development while retaining the existing zoning, which is a key difference between this tool and the mixed-use zoning districts or planned unit developments described in this toolkit. This type of overlay zone is particularly apt in established single-use areas with predominantly commercial, office, and retail uses to add a housing element while maintaining the code requirements that apply to nonresidential uses. Overlay zones can also be used strategically to encourage the construction of higher-density housing near transit stops (see also "Transit-Oriented Development" later in this toolkit).

Communities considering a mixed-use overlay zone should ensure adequate review standards for the newly allowed uses so they are applied consistently to projects within the zone. Overlay zones should be used selectively. If a risk exists of using overlays too frequently, overall rezoning may be more advisable to meet local land use needs.

## Examples and Resources

### Anaheim, California, Mixed-Use Overlay Zone
http://www.anaheim.net

In 2004, the city of Anaheim, California, adopted a mixed-use overlay zone for a 120-acre (48.56-hectare) area within a larger 820-acre (331.84-hectare) district zoned for industrial, office, and retail uses as a component of the Platinum Triangle Master Land Use Plan. The overlay zone sought to encourage adding market-driven mixed-use or higher-density residential projects to the mix while continuing to allow the existing uses. The overlay zone specifically instituted specific standards for desired residential development—such as density, open space, height limits, parking, and circulation—that would streamline the approvals process. At buildout, the area could include up to 9,500 dwelling units, 5 million square feet (464,515 square meters) of office space, and over 2 million square feet (185,806 square meters) of commercial uses.

### Maryland Smart Neighborhoods Model Ordinance
http://www.mdp.state.md.us/pdf/smartneighborhoods.pdf

The Maryland Department of Planning has produced *Smart Neighborhoods*, a model ordinance crafted as an overlay zone, to help local governments implement mixed-use and compact design without forgoing conventional zoning. It incorporates flexible use regulations, design guidelines, and a streamlined development review procedure.

### Salem, Oregon, Compact Development Overlay Zone
http://www.cityofsalem.net/~slegal/codes/ch139.pdf

To foster the development of a variety of housing types that are compatible with existing neighborhood character, the city of Salem, Oregon, adopted a compact development overlay zone to allow duplexes, triplexes, townhouses, and accessory dwelling units within areas that are otherwise zoned for single-family residential. The overlay zone allows a maximum density of up to 14 dwelling units per acre. The goal is to encourage the efficient use of land within the city's urban growth boundary, particularly infill opportunities on vacant or underused properties.

# Development Types

As more people are starting to realize the importance of living in higher density transit-accessible environments and as concepts such as smart growth and sustainability become more accepted, different development types and strategies are being pioneered to meet the demands. There have been numerous innovations in where and how new projects are developed. Developers and city officials alike have found that redeveloping brownfields or infill locations can reap large dividends both financially and in terms of improving citywide quality of life. Clustering buildings on a portion of a site allows developers to conserve open space. Tranist-oriented developments give people more opportunities to choose transit over cars, and traditional neighborhood developments demonstrate that living in high-density environments can be both beautiful and pedestrian-friendly.

## Brownfields Redevelopment

The reclamation of brownfields, land with a known or likely risk of environmental contamination, provides the opportunity to make productive use of abandoned or obsolete urban property. Although developers must address the risk of soil or water contamination from those previous uses, they can take advantage of various federal and state regulatory and financial incentive programs aimed at reclaiming brownfields for more-productive use. Often, urban centers have brownfields in prime locations that are now well situated for new residential or mixed-use development. They are often under single ownership, which eases the way for land assembly. By some estimates, some 5 million acres (2,023,428 hectares) of abandoned industrial property are located in U.S. urban areas.

Since its inception in 1995, the Brownfields Program of the U.S. Environmental Protection Agency (EPA) has grown into a proven, results-oriented program that has changed the way contaminated property is perceived, addressed, and managed. EPA's Brownfields Program is designed to empower states, communities, and other stakeholders in economic redevelopment to work together in a timely manner to prevent, assess, safely clean up, and reuse brownfields. The EPA defines *brownfields* as property whose expansion, redevelopment, or reuse may be complicated by the presence or potential presence of a hazardous substance, pollutant, or contaminant. More than 450,000 brownfields are estimated to exist in the United States. Cleaning up and reinvesting in these properties increases local tax bases, facilitates job growth, uses existing infrastructure, takes development pressures off undeveloped open land, and both improves and protects the environment.

Initially, EPA provided small amounts of seed money to local governments that launched hundreds of two-year brownfields "pilot" projects. Through passage of the Small Business Liability Relief and Brownfields Revitalization Act, effective polices that EPA had developed over the years were passed into law. The brownfields law expanded EPA's assistance by providing new tools for the public and private sectors to promote sustainable brownfields cleanup and reuse.

The EPA's Brownfields Program awards grants to support remediation and job training activities. In addition, many states have programs that channel funding for the assessment, cleanup, basic construction, and infrastructure development of brownfields sites.

Brownfields are frequently located in or near developed urban areas with infrastructure typically right up to the property line. Much in the way that infill development is well suited to higher-density residential development, brownfield sites are often well located for new urban uses, including multifamily residential development. Local and state government incentives, often in conjunction with federal grants, can provide the appropriate support for developers to undertake the effort. These efforts provide new housing opportunities, revitalize depressed communities, and remove environmental hazards.

## Keys to Success

The extent of the required environmental remediation is based on what use the cleaned-up property will be put to. Residential cleanup standards are, of course, the most rigorous. Rehabilitating a brownfield for housing development is usually a challenging and expensive job. The effort typically involves extensive public/private cooperation and various local, state, and federal agencies. Public and private partners may include local government agencies, developers, investors, real estate professionals, local community development corporations, citizens and community groups, state environmental agencies, state economic development and planning agencies, commercial lenders, technical consultants, legal counsel, and federal government agencies. Communities and developers seeking to redevelop brownfields, particularly for residential use, must be prepared to overcome the potential stigma associated with the site.

Because the costs of remediation can vary widely, the more that developers know about the level of contamination to be removed, the better the likelihood of presenting a viable property for brownfields reclamation. To foster brownfields redevelopment, some states and local governments have sought to assess contamination levels and estimate costs for cleanup.

Environmental insurance (EI) is growing in popularity and acceptance as a tool for redevelopment of these sites because of the unpredictable nature of brownfields reclamation. EI provides a means of transferring the risks inherent in the remediation of brownfields from private or public partners to an insurance firm. The three main types of EI policies for brownfields are pollution liability (to protect against future claims of harm related to contamination on remediated, redeveloped sites), cleanup cost cap (to provide a ceiling on cleanup costs), and secured lender (to protect a lender from borrower default related to a contamination factor). For more information on EI, see http://www.epa.gov/brownfields/insurebf.htm.

## Examples and Resources

### Pennsylvania Land Recycling Program
http://www.depweb.state.pa.us

In 1995, Pennsylvania initiated its land recycling program under its Department of Environmental Protection to encourage the voluntary cleanup and reuse of brownfields. The program is based on four elements that address barriers to redevelopment: uniform cleanup standards, liability relief, standardized reviews and time limits, and financial assistance that helps promote remediation and break down redevelopment obstacles.

### Pittsburgh's Washington Landing
http://www.ura.org/showcaseProjects_washLanding2.html

One brownfields site in Pennsylvania that has been redeveloped is Washington's Landing, in Pittsburgh. For more than a century, the 42-acre (17-hectare) Herr's Island on the Allegheny River was the site of industrial activity. Public and private investment of nearly $100 million in redevelopment of the site, renamed Washington's Landing, yielded a successful mixed-use community. The public funding supported land redevelopment, infrastructure, and cleanup efforts. The redeveloped property includes more than 100 residential units, a state agency, several commercial buildings with office space, several light-industrial manufacturing operations, a public park, and a restaurant.

### Northeast-Midwest Institute Survey
http://www.nemw.org/NAHBreport.pdf

In 2000, the Northeast-Midwest Institute released "Brownfields and Housing: How Are State VCPs Encouraging Residential Developments?" a report on the findings of a brownfields survey it conducted on behalf of the National Association of Home Builders to examine the potential for converting brownfields to residential development, particularly in light of state programs to support voluntary cleanup of these sites. The survey found that communities in many states were undertaking the residential reuse of brownfields, for example:

- California produced 5,200 new housing units on brownfields sites.
- Colorado developed 2,855 new units through its voluntary cleanup program.
- Michigan produced 1,400 new units at 11 different sites across the state.

## Cluster Development and Conservation Subdivision Design

Many of the land use and building codes to support compact development that this toolkit describes are most applicable to denser urban areas. However, greenfields are also a frequent development site in suburban and rural communities—and greenfields pose different challenges for supporting compact residential uses. Although not as complicated as infill or rehabilitation projects, greenfields have less existing infrastructure to support new development. Subdivisions in suburban

and rural settings are often governed by residential zoning regulations that encourage "sprawl": large minimum lot sizes and deep setbacks, wide road standards, and other provisions that result in low-density development.

*Conservation design* is an opportunity to allow development while also protecting the natural environment. Although conservation design has its origins in the eastern United States, it is being used in the west and other regions of the country. Conservation design clusters the development on a small portion of a site, protecting the most environmentally significant portions as open space. In some cases, as much as 80 percent of a site is protected.

*Cluster development* also preserves open space by grouping development, but on a smaller scale. The open space that cluster development preserves is usually considered common space that is managed by a homeowners association. Cluster development codes have been criticized for allowing conventional development types "by right" and also for allowing developers to take credit for preserving unbuildable land.

Regardless of the name, alternative zoning codes must provide tangible community benefits. Although cluster development and conservation subdivision design are often used synonymously, the latter is sometimes distinguished for its preeminent emphasis on land conservation and careful attention to high standards for the quantity, quality, and configuration of the resulting open space and developable area. Linkages between open spaces among adjacent subdivisions and existing parkland are also a key element in conservation subdivision design.

To produce cluster development, communities must revise local ordinances and regulations to indicate the design standards and specifications that apply to these projects. Some cluster development ordinances simply seek the development of less land area while allowing the same number of housing units that would otherwise be permitted. Others offer incentives such as density bonuses, particularly voluntary codes that allow developers to choose between standard subdivision regulations or those designed for cluster development.

## Keys to Success

Cluster development and conservation design have traditionally been most popular in rural areas seeking to preserve undeveloped landscapes. In addition to realizing the goal to reserve undeveloped land, these developments must encourage housing design that is compatible with the character of nearby communities, rather than simply transplant suburban housing types in a rural landscape. Design considerations can overcome the potential shortcomings of smaller lots, such as less privacy for homeowners. Appropriately written cluster development code streamlines construction and can provide design guidance to make the project a community asset.

## Examples and Resources

### Massachusetts Conservation Subdivision Design Project
http://www.mapc.org/regional_planning/land_use.html

Funded by the state Executive Office of Environmental Affairs, the greater Boston area Metropolitan Area Planning Council developed the Conservation Subdivision Design (CSD) Project in an effort to overcome negative perceptions and shortcomings of cluster development. The project created educational tools for planners, planning boards, and developers to broaden familiarity with the practice and encourage the widespread adoption of CSD. The three main outcomes of the CSD Project are

■ A detailed planning discussion of and commentary on the basic elements for consideration within a cluster-type open-space subdivision bylaw;

■ A Model Open Space Residential Design/CSD Bylaw and Model Subdivision Regulations; and

■ A casebook of four existing open space/cluster subdivisions in Massachusetts.

### Southeastern Wisconsin Model Zoning Ordinance for Rural Cluster Development
http://www.sewrpc.org/modelordinances/cluster_ordinance.pdf

The Southeastern Wisconsin Regional Planning Commission developed a model zoning ordinance for cluster development designed to guide communities seeking to implement local ordinances. The ordinance is designed as a mandatory district, which would require all residential development within the district to be clustered, and to preserve a minimum of 60 percent of the site as common open space.

### Conservation Design Books
http://www.greenerprospects.com/

Two popular resources for conservation design in local ordinances are *Conservation Design for Subdivisions: A Practical Guide to Creating Open Space Networks* and *Growing Greener: Putting Conservation into Local Plans and Ordinances*, both by Randall Arendt, a landscape planner. These books demonstrate how to lay out new neighborhoods where half to three-quarters of the land remains as permanent open space.

## Infill Development

Infill development is an opportunity to develop underused lots in established neighborhoods. It can also put vacant, blighted, or abandoned lots back into productive use through new development. As many communities face the reality of buildout, meaning all or most of their greenfield land has been developed, new infill development and redevelopment of existing parcels play an increasingly important role. Infill development plays a key role in smart growth and in creating sustainable communities and will continue to grow in importance as issues surrounding energy costs and availability, changing climate, and government-supported infrastructure edge closer to crisis. Infill redevelopment efforts are often directed to site-specific areas that may overlap with mixed-use zoning districts spread over larger, districtwide zones. The reuse of these parcels with new construction can help revitalize a declining area.

## How Can Infill Support Compact Development?

Infill development regulations can prioritize areas for desired projects and regulate the density, size, and design of new projects. Infill development is particularly effective when residential densities are sufficient to support multiple transportation options as well as a mix of commercial and retail uses.

A successful infill development program should contribute to neighborhood revitalization. Local regulations and building codes designed to encourage and guide infill development are critical to the successful redevelopment of infill sites, particularly because the site-specific issues for infill projects can require additional attention. In addition, communities may offer incentives to developers for new infill projects or seek to improve existing infrastructure to support such ventures.

## Examples and Resources

### Denver, Colorado, Regulatory Strategies for Encouraging Infill

http://www.drcog.org/documents/TODRegulatory%20 Strategies%20for%20Infill.pdf

In 2006, the Denver Regional Council of Governments published the report *Regulatory Strategies for Encouraging Infill and Redevelopment* to provide local governments with information about regulations that can support infill and redevelopment efforts. Techniques include assessing and adjusting zone districts to better facilitate infill and redevelopment, adopting mixed-use zoning codes and overlay districts, and assessing and modifying building codes.

### Maryland Models and Guidelines for Infill Development

http://www.mdp.state.md.us/mgs/infill/InfillFinal_1.pdf

The Maryland Department of Planning has produced the publication *Models and Guidelines for Infill Development*, which suggests rural, suburban, and urban strategies for infill development.

### Oregon Infill and Redevelopment Code Handbook

http://www.oregon.gov/LCD/docs/publications/ infilldevcode.pdf

The Oregon Transportation and Growth Management Program, a joint program of the Oregon Department of Transportation and the Oregon Department of Land Conservation and Development, has produced *The Infill and Redevelopment Code Handbook* to encourage infill and redevelopment in urban areas by identifying and removing barriers. Contents address the benefits and barriers to infill and redevelopment, a process for reviewing local conditions, and sample code language to remove regulatory barriers to infill.

## Traditional Neighborhood Development

Traditional neighborhood development (TND) ordinances allow the type of mixed-use development with architectural styles and a wide range of uses and housing types that were once common to pre–World War II neighborhoods in America. TND is generally implemented in a neighborhood of 10 to 15 acres (4.05 to 6.07 hectares) in an area based on a quarter-mile (.4-km) radius, at a scale that encourages a sense of place and a feeling of community for residents. The one-quarter-mile (.4-km) radius was chosen because that is the distance an average person can walk in ten minutes. Open space is typically 10 to 20 percent of the area, with about 70 to 80 percent of the area dedicated to residential uses; the remaining 10 percent or so is reserved for commercial/retail space and civic functions.

As with other types of mixed-use development, TND requires sufficient residential density to support the commercial and civic uses. TND projects can be developed in several ways, including redevelopment, infill, and greenfield sites. Locations near transportation infrastructure and employment hubs are particularly well suited for higher-density residential development. However, TND's emphasis on compact development with mixed uses means that greenfield projects are more likely to accommodate higher densities than would ordinarily be included when building new construction on undeveloped property.

### Keys to Success

Although TND is commonly associated with front porches, rear garages, and other aesthetic elements, several overarching characteristics are important for successful TND, including the following:

- A compact neighborhood with a variety of housing types and mix of uses;
- A connected street network that is accessible to pedestrians and bicycles as well as cars;
- Access to mass transit;
- Parks and public spaces spread throughout the neighborhood; and
- Architectural cohesiveness that contributes to a strong sense of place while also blending in with adjacent communities.

With the recognition of the essential elements of TND, local plans and zoning must support compatible street standards, parking ratios, densities, a mix of uses, and housing types. Clearly written regulatory code, particularly with ample graphics to illustrate preferred development patterns, is an important component of a successful TND project.

### Examples and Resources

**Maine Model Subdivision Regulations**
http://www.smrpc.org/landuse/subord/subord.htm

The most recent edition of Maine's *Model Subdivision Regulations*, produced by the Southern Maine Regional Planning Commission, seeks to incorporate smart growth considerations, such as traditional neighborhood design standards, access management, street and sidewalk design, and interconnectivity. It also is oriented to provide guidance for local planning boards that may be responsible for code revisions in smaller communities.

**Greensboro, North Carolina, Southside Neighborhood Redevelopment**
http://www.smartgrowth.org/library/articles.asp?art=1817

In 1999, the Greensboro, North Carolina, Department of Housing and Community Development developed a Traditional Neighborhood District Ordinance to assist with the redevelopment of ten acres (4.05 hectares) of the historic, but declining, Southside neighborhood in a mixed-use infill project. The ordinance was adopted to guide the project when the city realized its unified development ordinance would not support the new plan for traditional development that included smaller lots, zero setbacks, and mixed uses. A short walk from the central business district, the development includes 50 townhouses, 30 single-family homes, 20 live/work units, ten two-family homes, and ten restored historic homes. Several residences have accessory apartments above detached garages.

### Wisconsin TND Ordinance

http://dnr.wi.gov/org/es/science/landuse/
smart/SGlaw.htm

While many communities struggle with outdated or overly confining land use regulations that may inadvertently limit opportunities for compact development, the state of Wisconsin has sought to dismantle these local barriers with its *Smart Growth for Wisconsin* legislation. In 1999, Wisconsin passed the law to require all cities and villages above 12,500 in population to adopt a model TND ordinance, adapted to local needs and preferences, by 2010. As an effort to break down typical barriers to TND, the model ordinance supports the development of compact neighborhoods with a mix of residential, commercial, and civic uses. Under the law, communities may address TND as a zoning district designation, an overlay zone, a floating zone, or a modified approach to planned unit development. Much of the model ordinance provided as part of the legislation is devoted to specific design standards that address areas such as the following:

- Mix of land uses and housing types;
- Density of development;
- Open space;
- Building setbacks from sidewalks and lot lines;
- Transportation and pedestrian routes;

- Streets and parking;
- Architectural design of structures; and
- Lighting and landscaping.

## Transit-Oriented Development

Planned or existing transit systems—whether for buses, bus rapid transit, light rail, or heavy rail—are prime hubs for higher-density residential development. Known as transit-oriented development (TOD), it can increase public transit ridership; create pedestrian-friendly environments near transit stops; and encourage development of office, retail, entertainment, recreational, and civic functions. Many communities have found that local development codes and zoning do not readily allow for the compact development and reduced parking that is appropriate for TOD. Instead, local governments must adopt transit-oriented land use regulations to yield the benefits of TOD. These regulations can take a variety of forms, including the following:

- Different zoning classification: changing the TOD area to a more appropriate zoning category that will allow the desired uses and densities;
- Transit overlay zone: when current zoning requires only minor adjustments;
- New zoning district: creating a new district with its own land uses and development standards that can be tailored to the needs of the district; and
- Design guidelines: ensuring that TOD is compatible with the community.

### Why TOD?

Transit-oriented development is one of the most compelling rationales to promote compact development. Compact development provides the necessary density to support transit investment, creating viability for the transit system; studies indicate that adding residential housing choices within walking distance of a transit facility (a one-quarter to one-half mile [.4 to .8 km] radius, or up to a 15-minute walk) does more to increase transit usage than any other type of development. High-density residential development and other uses near a high-quality transit system can reduce car use and contribute to transit ridership.

The minimum residential density necessary to support regular bus service is about six to eight dwelling units per acre, according to the Victoria Transport Policy Institute. For express bus service with exclusively pedestrian access, average densities for the corridor should be about 15 dwelling units per acre. However, as densities increase, ridership increases. In fact, experts have reported a three-fold increase in ridership when average residential densities reach 30 units per acre. As further confirmation of the finding that transit stops benefit from proximity to high residential density, the Transportation Research Board has found that a resident in a mid-rise or high-rise multifamily neighborhood is 30 percent more likely to use transit than someone who lives in a single-family neighborhood. For transit stops near employment hubs, a minimum density of about 50 employees per acre is necessary to support regular transit service. Studies have found that people do not choose transit over driving until employment densities reach about 50 to 75 employees per acre.

## Keys to Success

Simply locating residential development adjacent to transit stops is often insufficient for successful TOD, particularly if the transit station is surrounded by surface parking. Land use and transportation planning must be well integrated. Etablishing design and use standards for an attractive, cohesive mixed-use area with nearby commercial, retail, and civic, as well as residential uses, is also important. Successful

transit-oriented development often benefits from changes in zoning codes and additional funding for pedestrian and bicycle facilities, which allow and encourage higher-density development around transit stations and reduce parking requirements.

## Examples and Resources

TOD efforts have been promoted at the state level as well as in regional and local efforts. New Jersey and Maryland are two states that have developed statewide strategies to promote TOD as infill around existing transit stations.

**Phoenix, Arizona, Comprehensive Program on Transit-Supportive Land Use**
http://www.valleymetro.org/Valley_Metro/Publications/Destinations/dest04fall.pdf

In anticipation of the opening of a new regional light-rail system in 2008, the city of Phoenix has sought to proactively encourage transit-supportive uses around designated transit stops before the Valley Metro Rail system is built. The city teamed with Valley Metro Rail, the Phoenix metropolitan area regional transit system, to encourage TOD near light-rail stations with a transit overlay zone near light-rail stations that encourages pedestrian-oriented uses and adapts the building code to support accessible housing. The city also undertook a market analysis to understand the development potential around the stations. The program aims to support surrounding development that is compatible with light rail and thus encourage use of the system. Anticipated ridership by 2020 is estimated to be 50,000 people daily.

### West Hyattsville, Maryland, Metro Transit District Development Plan
http://www.mncppc.org/cpd/westhyatts2.htm

The Maryland Department of Transportation (MDOT) has developed a TOD strategy designed to encourage the development of compact, mixed-use neighborhoods near transit stations, increase the number of transit riders, and enhance the return on its investment in this infrastructure. MDOT efforts have included sponsoring station area planning studies, soliciting development proposals for surplus right-of-way property near transit stations, and locating stations to maximize opportunities for TOD and economic development.

In the Washington, D.C., suburb of West Hyattsville, Maryland, MDOT brought together local elected officials, planning and zoning staff and commissions, resource and public works agency staff, landowners, neighbors, and others to develop a strategy for the local Metrorail station. The strategy is intended to attract and guide high-quality development at this site as well as at all of Prince George's County's 14 other Metrorail stations. In addition to extensive stakeholder involvement, the strategic planning process included a site analysis, a market analysis, a review of existing policies and regulations, and a consideration of financial issues. The process also included a developers' forum to gather private sector comment on this plan and ensure that it accurately reflected local development realities. The final plan calls for a low-rise (two- to six-story) community that features 3,600 residential units in a variety of housing types; 1 million square feet (92,902 square meters) of office and commercial space; a system of civic, park, and open spaces; and a carefully planned street and circulation network.

### New Jersey Transit Village Initiative
http://www.state.nj.us/transportation/community/village

New Jersey's statewide Transit Village Initiative is a multiagency partnership headed by the New Jersey Department of Transportation (NJDOT) and New Jersey Transit. The program aims to encourage residential and retail development around existing transit facilities, reduce traffic congestion, and improve air quality by reducing automobile vehicle miles traveled. Communities can apply to become designated a Transit Village, which yields benefits such as priority funding and technical assistance from certain state agencies, eligibility for grants from NJDOT's Transit Village funding, and coordination among the state agencies on the Transit Village task force. To qualify for designation as a Transit Village, municipalities must be dedicated to developing compact, mixed-use neighborhoods with a strong residential component around their transit facility. Since 1999, 17 rail-oriented and bus-oriented urban and suburban New Jersey communities have been designated as Transit Villages.

### Huntersville, North Carolina, Transit-Oriented Development Code
www.Huntersville.org

In anticipation of future transit stations planned in Huntersville, North Carolina, which is outside Charlotte, the city adopted a development code that encourages higher-density housing and employment hubs within a five-minute walk of stops planned on the proposed "North Corridor" leg of the Charlotte Area Transit System rapid-transit line. Although this transit corridor is not yet under construction (the first branch is the 9.6-mile [15.45 km] South Corridor line, scheduled to open in fall 2007), it has provided the city with a means to direct transit-oriented compact development around the proposed transit line.

### Portland, Oregon, Central City Transportation Management Plan

http://www.portlandonline.com/transportation/index.cfm?a=bfaeed&c=dgijj

To encourage concentrated growth in central Portland, the city developed its *Central City Transportation Management Plan* as the principal planning document guiding transportation policies in the central city. The plan promotes mixed-use and higher-density development to reduce regional vehicle travel. The plan considers parking management, transit service, pedestrian and bicycle improvements, and traffic circulation improvements.

### Salt Lake City, Utah, TOD Overlay

http://www.envisionutah.org/resourcesfiles/22/South%20Salt%20Lake%20TOD%20Code.doc

South Salt Lake City has developed a transit-oriented overlay district with incentives to encourage property owners to apply TOD principles to the development of land near the TRAX light-rail stations and transit stops. Incentives include more permitted and conditional use options, increased densities and building height, decreased setbacks, and decreased parking requirements.

### Burlington, Vermont, Transit-Oriented Design Manual

http://www.ccrpcvt.org/

Design guidance can often provide a definitive visual example of desired development that is useful for encouraging desired outcomes in TOD. In Burlington, Vermont, the Chittenden County Regional Planning Commission published *Transit-Oriented Design (TOD) for Chittenden County: Guidelines for Planners, Policymakers, Developers and Residents* in 2002. The guidelines show developers and municipalities how large- and small-scale real estate development projects can serve transit users.

The guidebook also demonstrates to planners and designers specific site-planning and design elements that may be included in their plans to foster successful transit-oriented developments.

### Rosslyn-Ballston Corridor, Arlington County, Virginia

http://www.smartgrowth.org/library/articles.asp?art=1824&res=1024

Since Metrorail's inception 30 years ago, planners in the Arlington County, Virginia, suburb of Washington, D.C., have promoted transit-oriented development around the county's five Metrorail stations, known as the Rosslyn-Ballston Corridor. In addition to requiring compact, mixed-use development at the stations, the county's general land use plan provides sector plans to distinguish each station and incentive zoning to attract private sector development. The result has been the development of active urban-transit villages with high-density residential properties, retail and commercial uses, and pedestrian activity concentrated over the two-square-mile (5.18-km) area. As of 2004, the corridor had nearly 25,000 residential units; 21 million square feet (1,950,964 square meters) of office, retail, and commercial space; and more than 3,000 hotel rooms. Nearly half of corridor residents commute by transit.

### Metropolitan Seattle, Washington, Transit Station Communities Project

http://www.psrc.org/projects/tod/index.htm

On a regional level, the Seattle-area Puget Sound Regional Council has initiated a Transit Station Communities for commuter-rail stations serving smaller communities between Seattle and Tacoma, Washington. The Metropolitan Planning Organization was able to share its regional planning expertise with local governments in this effort.

# Density and Design Tools

Encouraging density and compact development requires a wide-ranging and flexible set of tools. The following are a selection of tools that can facilitate denser developments. Accessory housing and cottage housing both work by increasing the number of units and people in an area. Design review and guidelines help by establishing rules for developers, contractors, and architects to follow when trying to encourage higher-density development. Rating systems can provide metrics for assessing whether projects meet a predetermined set of outcomes. Financial incentives come in a variety of forms and can be crucial for creating "buy-in" from the private sector. Transportation demand management and street classification systems are very important in managing how parking and traffic affect an area.

## Accessory Housing and Cottage Housing

Adapting local zoning codes to include accessory housing and cottage housing can yield more compact development—as well as more affordable housing—in existing communities. Accessory housing, also known as garage apartments, granny flats, or in-law apartments, consists of secondary housing units located on the same site as a single-family residence. In neighborhoods that are otherwise zoned for single-family housing, regulations can be revised to permit accessory housing units.

Cottage housing units are detached single-family houses that are smaller than average (600 to 1,000 square feet [56 to 93 square meters]) and are typically sited in clusters of four to 20 units to share a common area or other amenities. The concept of cottage housing is alternately referred to as small lot subdivisions, bungalow courts, and other names that all refer to the basic idea of creating small

single-family homes sited together with common areas. These smaller-than-average houses can offer a less-expensive housing choice at a higher density as well as viable infill that nonetheless maintains the character of established neighborhoods.

### How Does It Work?

In established neighborhoods of single-family houses where there is an urgent need for more affordable housing or a demand for a greater variety of housing types, accessory housing and cottage housing can provide an ideal infill solution. Municipalities often adopt a specific ordinance to permit either of these types of development and allow a level of density in areas otherwise zoned for single-family residential on larger lots.

As an effort to provide more housing choices at higher densities, accessory housing or cottage housing units are typically incorporated into an existing neighborhood. Thus, good communication with current residents is important when adopting an ordinance or code to allow these types of development, to allow public comment and review of the proposed zoning changes.

### Examples and Resources

Municipalities such as Santa Cruz, California; Barnstable, Massachusetts; and Falmouth, Maine, have adopted regulations to allow accessory housing units in an effort to provide more housing options in single-family residential neighborhoods.

The town of Langley, Washington, on Whidbey Island in Puget Sound, was one of the first municipalities to adopt its Cottage Housing Development Code in 1995. The code permits up to 12 units per acre—twice the density that would otherwise be allowed. Since then, other Washington cities, including Seattle, Redmond, and Shoreline, have passed cottage housing zoning.

### Los Angeles Small Lot Subdivision Ordinance
http://cityplanning.lacity.org/Code_Studies/Housing/smalllotpolicyFINAL.pdf

Los Angeles has one of the most expensive housing markets in the country, in part because of basic rules of supply and demand. In response, the city of Los Angeles adopted the small lot subdivision ordinance, which allows individuals or developers to purchase a lot zoned for commercial or multifamily residential and subdivide the property into smaller lots than previously required. The ordinance does not require setbacks and eliminates the need for numerous variances that would previously have been required; it encourages infill development in existing communities close to jobs and existing infrastructure.

### Santa Cruz, California, Accessory Dwelling Unit Development Program
http://www.ci.santa-cruz.ca.us/pl/hcd/ADU/adu

The state of California enacted a law requiring municipalities to permit accessory units. The city of Santa Cruz responded with one of the best programs in the state, the comprehensive Accessory Dwelling Unit (ADU) Development Program. In addition to legalizing ADUs in the zoning code, the city created a popular "how to" manual for residents considering building an accessory unit on their property. The city also pre-reviewed seven 500-square-foot (46-square-meter) homes created by architects to reduce design costs and simplify approvals. City officials expect 30 to 40 new units to be constructed each year.

### ADUs: Model State Act and Local Ordinance
http://assets.aarp.org/rgcenter/consume/d17158_dwell.pdf.

In 2000, AARP and the American Planning Association issued "Accessory Dwelling Units: Model State Act and Local Ordinance," a report on ADUs that includes both a model state act and local zoning ordinance for ADUs.

## Design Review and Design Guidelines

Including community-based design guidelines and design review as part of the zoning code offers communities an opportunity to shape the aesthetic of compact development and ensures that it is consistently compatible with local character. Elements of design review include streetscapes, building mass and scale, architectural details, setbacks, facades, landscaping, configuration of public spaces, safety and security, and signage. Design guidelines often are discretionary, whereas design standards usually provide no discretion in decision making and impose measurable, clear, and objective standards. Knowing whether guidelines or standards are the appropriate method of design review is a matter of context and judgment on the part of the local community.

Design considerations can be particularly important in the more intimate spaces of compact development, which will be more frequently experienced at a human scale than automobile-oriented development. Attractive design is frequently an important asset for market appeal as well as overall public acceptance of high-density development.

## Keys to Success

Successful design considerations for higher density housing include the following:

- Walkability, provided by wide sidewalks, short street blocks, and slower car traffic;
- A mix of stores, offices, restaurants, schools, libraries, and other commercial, retail, and civic choices that contribute to a lively street throughout the day and evening;
- Zero or minimal setbacks and interesting transparent facades that create an intimate streetscape;
- Welcoming parks and public spaces and landscaping—amenities that residents of higher-density development enjoy because of the concentration of housing elsewhere on site;
- Balancing architectural consistency while allowing for creativity;
- Balancing overall regulatory flexibility and prescription;
- Clarity on what aspects of design are subject to review and by what standards; and
- Clarity on the composition of any design review committee, its authority, and the applicability and process for the design review.

## Examples and Resources

### Fort Collins, Colorado, Design Manual
http://fcgov.com/advanceplanning/design-manual.php

The city of Fort Collins, Colorado, has sought to encourage compact development in its land use codes. However, local planners have also realized the effectiveness of using pictures to convey the intention of the land development regulations. As a result, the city of Fort Collins has produced an illustrated design manual that is cross-referenced to its land development code to show the desired results of these regulations.

### GrowSmart Maine Design Principles
http://www.maine.gov/spo/landuse/

The Maine State Planning Office and GrowSmart Maine published the report, *The Great American Neighborhood: Contemporary Design Principles for Building Livable Residential Communities*, in 2004. One of a series of publications addressing sprawl, the report suggests design ideas and principles that residential developers, homebuilders, and town officials can apply to create attractive traditional neighborhoods that appeal to current market demands. Topics covered include site selection, project planning, grid, block and street design, lot layout, and home siting and design.

### NorthPoint in Cambridge, Massachusetts
http://www.northpointcambridge.com/

The 45-acre (18.21-hectare) mixed-use NorthPoint development, in Cambridge, Massachusetts, is a major infill project located on a former rail yard. At completion, the project will have 20 buildings containing 2.2 million square feet (204,387 square meters) of commercial space and 2,700 residential units as well as ten acres (4.05 hectares) of green space, close to regional light-rail lines. The project broke ground in 2005 for two condominium buildings and a five-acre (2.02-hectare) park. The character and design of the project are guided by North Point Design Guidelines, an area-specific portion of the Eastern Cambridge Design Guidelines. The guidelines govern specifications for details such as building heights, lot sizes, and the street network, as well as overall image, scale, character, and links with other neighborhoods.

**Blackstone River Valley Design Review Manual**

http://www.nps.gov/archive/blac/what/DRManualdocument_web.pdf

Aimed at historic Rhode Island and Massachusetts communities in the Blackstone River Valley, this publication shares general information on how design review works and how to begin a local design review process. The manual shows how localities can develop an architectural assessment ordinance to guide the appearance of new structures, uses, and signs. It includes designation of local historic districts, review of site plans, and how to implement design review.

**Salem, Oregon, Development Design Handbook**

http://www.ci.salem.or.us/export/departments/scdev/cityplan/Development_Design_Handbook.pdf

The *Development Design Handbook* provides an introduction to the city's development design process, outlines the design requirements for multifamily development, identifies the requirements for compact development, contains requirements for the core area, covers historic resources, and addresses specific design guidelines for designated districts in the city. The Salem development design process applies to all new multifamily and compact development projects, projects in the core downtown, historic resources throughout the city, the north downtown planning district, and two designated neighborhood overlay zones.

Furthermore, Salem's handbook explains the city's design review process, in which the developer may choose whether to have the project proposal reviewed by the Historic Landmarks and Design Review Commission or to have the proposal evaluated based on compliance with conventional development standards.

■ If the applicant chooses review by the Historic Landmarks and Design Review Commission, the project review is based on clearly defined *design guidelines* that address elements such as open space, landscaping, parking, site access, and building massing as well as all city code requirements. These decisions require public notice, and the final decision is subject to appeal to the State Land Use Board of Appeals.

■ Projects not reviewed by the Historic Landmarks and Design Review Commission are subject to compliance with *design standards* and all city code requirements. Design standards address the same project elements as design guidelines; however, they provide no discretion in decision making and are measurable, clear, and objective. Because project review based on measurable standards involves no discretion (either a project proposal meets the standards or it does not), this type of project review does not require public notice or hearing.

## Development Rating Systems

To encourage more-compact, efficient forms of development, some communities have created a rating system, or scorecard, to evaluate development projects. Some rating systems become a decision-making tool, especially when implemented at the local level. In many cases, a project must achieve a high ranking to be eligible for incentives such as expedited review. For example, the city of Austin, Texas, designed the Smart Growth Criteria Matrix in 1999 as a tool to assist the city council's evaluation of certain development proposals. The matrix considers the location of development, its proximity to mass transit, urban design characteristics, density thresholds, neighborhood support, employment opportunities, increased tax base, and other policy priorities. A high-scoring project may be eligible for financial incentives, such as the reduction or elimination of development fees or public infrastructure investment. See http://www.ci.austin.tx.us/smartgrowth/smartmatrix.htm for more information.

In other cases, nonprofit organizations may create a rating scale to evaluate projects and provide a desired "seal of approval" to high-scoring proposals. In either case, the rating process highlights the most desirable features, such as location, density, access to transit, design features, and landscaping. The Washington Smart Growth Alliance (a collaborative partnership of which the Urban Land Institute's Washington District Council is a member) established the Smart Growth Recognition Program to help promote worthy projects and smooth the approval process in the Washington, D.C., region. An appointed jury reviews submitted project proposals and selects those to endorse smart growth developments. The criteria include location; density, design, and diversity of uses; multimodal transportation access; environment; mixed-income housing; and community assets. For more information, see www.sgalliance.org.

## Keys to Success

Ease of application and credibility are probably the most important factors in an effective development rating system. For systems used by local governments, developers submitting proposals will appreciate clear guidelines for preferred project characteristics and an easily comprehensible method of evaluation. For ratings criteria advanced by private nonprofits, establishing credibility, creating an effective method for publicizing the high-scoring projects, and garnering community support are also important to encourage developers to submit project proposals for review.

## Examples and Resources

**Mobile, Alabama, Smart Growth Policy Document**
http://www.cityofmobile.org/pdf/PolicyExecutiveSummary.pdf

In an effort to encourage higher-density, pedestrian-friendly redevelopment, the city of Mobile approved a package of smart growth guidelines with a variety of incentives that would apply to developments throughout the city. Eligible features include grid-pattern streets, alleyways, on-street parking, shared driveway entrances, alternative driveway surfaces, proximity to transit, buildings close to streets, tree removal only if absolutely necessary, walking and biking trails, and mixed land uses. Incentives include expedited review, reduction or waiver of permit and application fees, a waiver of city sales tax on construction materials, and other financial inducements.

**San Francisco Greenbelt Alliance Compact Development Endorsement Program**
http://www.greenbelt.org/whatwedo/prog_cdt_index.html

In California, the San Francisco area Greenbelt Alliance has a Compact Development Endorsement Program, which aims to encourage high-quality projects and make the development process easier for developers. Residential, mixed-use, and commercial developments are eligible for consideration. The program criteria include housing affordability, pedestrian friendliness, and project density. After meeting the criteria, a developer receives a letter of support and active endorsement at public hearings and other forums.

### Silicon Valley Leadership Group Home Development Endorsement Criteria
http://www.svmg.org/issues/housing/resources/200601homedev_endorsement.pdf

The Silicon Valley Leadership Group (SVLG), founded in 1977 in San Jose, California, is a business association of more than 200 member companies that constitute a major portion of the area's economy. The SVLG was organized to foster collaboration between the leadership of member businesses and local, regional, state, and federal government officials to address major public policy matters, such as affordable housing, transportation, high-quality schools, and other issues affecting regional economic health and quality of life.

The SVLG's Home Development Endorsement Criteria support project proposals that discourage urban sprawl, provide for mixed-use development, realize the construction of more compact development within urbanized areas of the valley, and encourage the use of transit. The criteria also include specific measures for features such as appropriate location, scale, density, traffic, and affordability. For example, density criteria indicate that "Proposed developments must include at least 20 homes per acre if located with a quarter-mile radius of a rail station and at least 12 homes per acre within a half-mile radius of a rail or major bus station." If the SVLG endorses a proposed development, the organization will provide a letter of support and public testimony from SVLG staff.

### State of Maryland Smart Growth Scorecard
http://www.smartgrowth.state.md.us/score.htm

Maryland's Office of Smart Growth uses a scorecard to evaluate projects around the state and offer assistance that can improve smart growth features. Created in collaboration with several state agencies, the scorecard considers a project's location, services, density and compactness, mixed use, housing diversity, transportation, community character and design, environmental protection, stakeholder participation, and economic development.

### New Jersey Smart Growth Scorecard
http://www.njfuture.org

New Jersey Future, a statewide nonprofit research and policy organization, has developed two scorecards designed to evaluate smart growth potential. The Smart Growth Scorecard for Proposed Developments is a project-specific assessment tool designed to rate development proposals based on smart growth criteria developed by the organization. These criteria include location, a range of housing options, protection of environmental areas and open space, development of mixed uses, transportation options, pedestrian friendliness, and incorporation of appropriate community character. The Municipal Planning Scorecard is based on the same general criteria but instead focuses on whether a municipality's land use and zoning laws can support these qualities in new developments.

### Vermont Smart Growth Collaborative Housing Endorsement Program

http://www.vnrc.org/article/articleview/5397/1/650/

In 2001, the nonprofit Vermont Smart Growth Collaborative, in collaboration with the Vermont Housing and Conservation Board, Housing Vermont, and other housing organizations, created a the Housing Endorsement Program. The voluntary endorsement program seeks to encourage residential development based on smart growth principles. High-ranking projects earn a Vermont Smart Growth Collaborative endorsement that can be submitted for consideration during planning and permitting review. The criteria for endorsement include creating a compact, mixed-use development at an appropriate scale for the community and the region; offering a choice in modes of transportation; protecting natural and historic resources; strengthening or minimizing conflict with agricultural and forest industries; balancing growth with available infrastructure; supporting local business; and providing housing that meets the needs of a diversity of households.

## Financial Incentives

While rating systems seek to provide a variety of incentives that can smooth the development process, other programs have dedicated funds to encourage desired forms of development. Compact development is an integral outcome of these sources of funding or services, but the actual sources of these funds are often allocated on the basis of transportation planning concerns. A state or regional agency often awards financial incentives to localities. Awards take on a variety of forms, including the following:

■ *Grants to municipalities to produce specific plans that support desired types of development:* Since 1995, the localities in the greater Twin Cities metropolitan area have applied for funds under the Livable Communities Act, a state grant program developed to support economic revitalization, affordable housing efforts, and development that links land use and transportation. Atlanta's Livable Centers Initiative, administered by the Atlanta Regional Commission, awards planning grants to local governments and nonprofit organizations to support higher-density residential development, mixed uses, and transportation connectivity consistent with regional development policies.

■ *Statewide bond initiatives:* The voters of the state of California recently approved state bonds that include $850 million in grants for infrastructure improvements that will support compact development. Such investment in infrastructure can spur appropriate development and redevelopment in areas targeted for growth, especially areas served by public transportation.

■ *Funds determined on a per unit basis:* Developed to encourage communities to adopt a higher-density overlay zone, the Massachusetts Chapter 40R Smart Growth Overlay includes funding based on the number of units produced. In California, the City/County Association of Governments of San Mateo County operates a countywide transit-oriented development incentive program that awards funds for high-density units built near transit stations, a program that has been copied in San Francisco.

■ *Technical assistance to implement plans, often in conjunction with financial support:* The Massachusetts Chapter 40R program includes technical assistance to help localities with code revisions. The Albany, New York, Community and Transportation Linkage Planning Program offers an in-kind awards to communities by providing staff or private consultant technical support for local planning efforts to coordinate land use and transportation planning.

## How Can Financial Incentives Support Compact Development?

Tying financial rewards to higher-density residential construction is probably one of the most direct ways to yield the desired type of development. This kind of carrot can also provide opportunities to leverage other desired outcomes, such as housing affordable to a mix of incomes. For each community, the exact nature of the program will differ, depending on local needs and conditions. The financial incentive may actually come in the form of a fee reduction based on a sliding scale of density or some other development aspect desired by the community, including affordability.

Financial incentives are a powerful tool to encourage the adoption of appropriate planning and zoning to achieve higher densities and to provide opportunities to build such projects in communities that might not otherwise be receptive to the prospect. The financial compensation also mitigates the burden of additional time or effort involved in making necessary changes to zoning code or developing a visionary plan. In addition to providing funding, which can take the form of infrastructure investment, land grants, fee waivers, tax abatements, and other tools that reduce the overall cost of developing compact development, providing technical assistance is a useful component that helps ensure the success of such efforts.

### Examples and Resources

**San Mateo County, California, TOD Incentive Program**
http://www.smartgrowth.org/library/articles.asp?art=1827&res=1024

In San Mateo County, California, commutes were getting longer as affordable housing became more distant from jobs. To address the problem, in 1999 the City/County Association of Governments (C/CAG) of San Mateo County started a countywide transit-oriented development incentive program to encourage local land use authorities to develop housing near transit stations. The incentive allows C/CAG to designate up to 10 percent of its state transportation improvement program funds to such projects. Density must be at least 40 units per acre, and housing must be within one-third of a mile (.53 km) of a rail transit station to be eligible for the program, which offers transportation funding grants of up to $2,000 per bedroom for applicable housing projects. Additionally, the grant program offers up to $2,250 per bedroom for applicable projects that include a minimum of 10 percent of the units at low- and moderate-income levels. Between 1999 and 2004, the program supported the construction of nearly 4,000 units.

**San Francisco Housing Incentive Program**
http://www.mtc.ca.gov/

The San Mateo program inspired the creation of the San Francisco Metropolitan Transportation Commission's similar Housing Incentive Program, which has been in place since 2000. The commission allocates regional transportation funds to foster the development of high-density housing projects near mass transit stations.

**Atlanta, Georgia, Livable Centers Initiative**
http://www.atlantaregional.com/cps/rde/xchg/arc/hs.xsl/308_ENU_HTML.htm

Atlanta's Livable Centers Initiative (LCI), administered by the Atlanta Regional Commission (ARC), encourages localities in the 18-county ARC region to support denser residential development, mixed land uses, and connectivity to encourage transit, bicycle, and pedestrian trips and reduce automobile vehicle miles traveled. The program awards planning grants to local governments and nonprofit organizations on a competitive basis to support the linkage of transportation improvements with land use development strategies consistent with regional development policies. The program's principal goals are to

- Encourage a compact mix of land uses;
- Provide access to a range of travel modes, including transit, roadways, walking, and biking; and
- Develop an outreach process to involve all stakeholders.

Since 2000, ARC has approved a total of $10 million over ten years to fund the study portion of the program. ARC also approved $500 million for priority funding of transportation projects resulting from the LCI studies. To date, more than 40 cities, towns, and suburban subcenters have been funded for an LCI study.

### Massachusetts Smart Growth Overlay
http://www.mass.gov/envir/smart_growth_toolkit/pages/mod-40R.html

In 2005, the commonwealth of Massachusetts adopted Chapter 40R to allow cities and towns to establish special "smart growth" zoning overlay districts and provide technical assistance and financial incentives to do so. Administered by the Department of Housing and Community Development (DHCD), the overlay district allows densities of 20 units per acre for condominiums and apartments, 12 units per acre for townhouses, and eight units per acre for single-family homes. The zoning district must require that 20 percent of homes be affordable and must allow a mixed-use combination of residential, office, and retail nearby. The goal of the overlay zones is to encourage compact development and higher-density housing in town centers, in downtowns, near transit stations, on unused industrial land, or in other locations municipalities approved for this type of development. The DHCD must approve the proposed district.

The state assists municipalities in writing applicable bylaw revisions to add the district to the local zoning ordinance, as well as in planning and design. In addition, cities and towns can receive between $10,000 and $600,000 in state funding, plus an additional $3,000 for every new home created in exchange for adopting the overlay zone and facilitating the development process under Chapter 40R.

As of spring 2007, ten municipalities had received approval for applications for 40R districts, and eight more were seeking or pending approval from the DHCD. These districts would create a combined total of 6,118 dwelling units with 1,223 affordable units.

### Minneapolis–St. Paul Livable Communities Act
http://www.metrocouncil.org/services/livcomm.htm

In 1995, the Minnesota state legislature established the Livable Communities Grant Program, a voluntary, incentive-based grant program for the greater Twin Cities metropolitan area, to support community economic revitalization efforts, affordable housing initiatives, and development that links different land uses and transportation. Administered by the Metropolitan Council of Minneapolis–St. Paul, grants to participating communities in the seven-county region range from $10,000 to $150,000 and may be awarded under three separate accounts:

- Tax Base Revitalization Account, for brownfields reclamation and redevelopment;
- Local Housing Incentive Account, administered in cooperation with the Minnesota Housing Finance Agency to produce and preserve low- and moderate-income housing; and

■ Livable Communities Demonstration Account, to support development projects that connect housing, jobs, and services.

Since its creation, the program has supported more than 23,000 new and 600 rehabilitated housing units in 47 communities. It has funded the production of 2,000 new affordable rental units, 600 rehabilitated rental units, and 800 affordable new and rehabilitated ownership units. In the first ten years, the program awarded more than 400 grants totaling over $160 million.

**Albany, New York, Community and Transportation Linkage Planning Program**
http://www.cdtcmpo.or

The Albany, New York–based Capital District Transportation Committee launched its Community and Transportation Linkage Planning Program in 2000 to encourage the coordination of land use and transportation planning. The program provides communities with staff or private consultant technical support for local planning efforts. These joint collaborations strive to implement the regional transportation plan, which seeks to reduce auto dependence in the metropolitan area through local land use plans, highway and transit designs, zoning ordinances, pedestrian and bicycle accommodation, and other means. The program has dedicated $3.3 million in local, state, and federal funds since 2000 and produced a total of 55 land use and transportation studies in 30 urban, suburban, and rural communities through 2006.

# Transportation Demand Management

Carefully designing parking facilities as well as managing overall transportation choices is a critical component to attractive, walkable compact development. In part, this development can be achieved by reducing the need for parking, which is a natural consequence of decreased car dependency and access to walking, transit, and other modes of transportation. Most communities that have some form of environmental review process require transportation demand management (TDM) for larger development proposals.

## How Can TDM Support Compact Development?

New high-density development results in new transportation demands. A TDM plan can encourage a wide variety of mobility options and steer commuters away from overloaded modes, generally driving alone in cars. TDM policies can include pricing and location of parking, ready access to public transit, nearby convenience retail, and even bike parking and shower facilities to facilitate bike commuting. In addition, studies have shown that residents of multifamily buildings have fewer cars and make fewer trips than residents of single-family homes. This fact means that flexible parking standards can reduce the need for additional surface spaces by managing parking needs with techniques such as shared parking, reduced parking ratios, and siting parking spaces discreetly behind buildings or curbside. Compact mixed-use development makes possible "park once" policies where one parking space is used for a variety of errands.

## Examples and Resources

### Victoria, British Columbia, Transport Policy Institute TDM Encyclopedia
http://www.vtpi.org/tdm/

The Victoria Transport Policy Institute maintains a comprhenensive TDM encyclopedia that includes a wide variety of TDM strategies, policies, and resources. The resource is regularly updated with new examples and policies.

### Arlington County, Virginia, TDM Policy
http://www.commuterpage.com/TDM/

Arlington County, Virgnia, has required that developers seeking site plan approval for new projects in the county complete a Transportation Demand Management Plan. The county encourages tenants to offer transit benefits, buildings to provide bike facilities, and structured parking to be priced and open to the public.

---

### TEN PRINCIPLES TO SUPPORT PARKING MANAGEMENT

1. **Consumer choice.** People should have viable parking and travel options.

2. **User information.** Motorists should have information on their parking and travel options.

3. **Sharing.** Parking facilities should serve multiple users and destinations.

4. **Efficient utilization.** Parking facilities should be sized and managed so spaces are frequently occupied.

5. **Flexibility.** Parking plans should accommodate uncertainty and change.

6. **Prioritization.** The most desirable spaces should be managed to favor higher-priority uses.

7. **Pricing.** As much as possible, users should pay directly for the parking facilities they use.

8. **Peak management.** Special efforts should be made to deal with peak demand.

9. **Quality vs. quantity.** Parking facility quality should be considered as important as quantity, including aesthetics, security, accessibility, and user information.

10. **Comprehensive analysis.** All significant costs and benefits should be considered in parking planning.

*Source:* Todd Litman, *Parking Management Strategies, Evaluation and Planning*, Victoria Transport Policy Institute, 2006.

## Street Classification and Design

*Street classification* is a method of categorizing streets according to the level of service they are intended to provide to users, often with an emphasis on motor vehicles. Classification is a means to inform the people who use the street, the people who live on the street, and the planners who work with the street designs and land use what level of vehicle traffic and other activity to expect. The urban street classifications used by federal, state, and local agencies generally consist of five groups:

1. Expressways;
2. Arterials;
3. Major collectors;
4. Minor collectors; and
5. Local streets.

Some municipalities have sought to broaden traditional functional street classification to better address the needs of pedestrians, cyclists, and transit users. For example, the city and county of Denver, Colorado, decided to revise its street classification system with considerations for their actual function. In addition to arterial streets, collector streets, and local streets, the system designates a new multimodal street classification called "downtown access streets" that serve dense mixed-use areas within the downtown. In an effort to help city planners characterize streets more precisely, Denver has created five street typologies: residential, main, mixed-use, commercial, and industrial. These descriptors can be used to modify particular classifications, such as "mixed-use arterial" or "residential collector."

*Street design* refers to the aesthetic and functional standards that apply to streets, such as widths, landscaping in the right-of-way, sidewalks, and lighting. Street design that supports the goals of a walkable, mixed-use community includes considerations of street and block pattern, street hierarchy, pavement width, streetscape features, and street-oriented building facades.

### How Can Street Classification and Design Support Compact Development?

Street design and higher densities have an interdependent relationship. Although multifamily properties can and do exist along automobile-oriented, high-speed streets with minimal pedestrian or transit access, flexible street design standards that allow narrower widths, pedestrian- and bicycle-friendly design, and on-street parking can create a more-hospitable environment for multifamily housing. Street design in local development regulations should reflect the scale of individual neighborhoods and types of traffic the streets carry. Codes should ensure that neighborhood streets are designed appropriately to create attractive, navigable corridors that include street trees, adequate sidewalks, transit shelters, and bike parking, as well as carefully accommodating automobile traffic flow and allowing on-street parking. In addition to design considerations, innovative approaches to street classifications can help reflect more accurately the needs of multiple users. More sensitively designed transportation networks that provide a variety of transportation choices are a better match for high-density residential buildings and offer a higher quality of life.

## Keys to Success

Modifying street design standards will affect a variety of stakeholders, such as local officials, neighborhood groups, landowners, and developers, who should be included in the undertaking. The process typically includes examining current street design standards and comparing them to more flexible street design guidelines to determine what changes would be appropriate. Local police, fire, and public works departments may have concerns that need to be addressed. Examples of safety and maintenance issues include access by ambulances, fire trucks, and snow plows. Obviously, a hierarchy of streets must exist, based on the anticipated use of the roadways. Data from existing new urbanist communities with narrower streets can be useful in making the case that safety and maintenance can be addressed on narrower streets.

## Good Examples

Some communities have used street design and classifications as a cornerstone for encouraging compact development. In Cornelius, North Carolina, the land development code has a strong pedestrian emphasis with detailed landscaping and sidewalk requirements. These considerations affect the streetscape and local building design.

When Plantation, Florida, designed the new zoning code for the Plantation Midtown District, the four different street classifications—ranging from small-scale urban to major suburban arterial—were the underlying factor in determining allowable building height and bulk.

---

### ELEMENTS OF SMART STREET DESIGN

- An interconnected street and block pattern that provides many routes for travel in the neighborhood and mitigates the effect of automobile traffic. Block lengths are between 300 and 800 feet (91.44 and 243.84 meters), with an average of 500 feet (152.4 meters). Alleys can provide rear garage access and eliminate curb cuts and driveways on the street.

- A hierarchy of streets within the interconnected grid with right-of-way width, pavement width, number of lanes, sidewalks, landscaping, and design speed clearly described.

- Streetscape features, such as sidewalks, street trees and other landscaping, lighting and crosswalks, shown with clear graphics. Sidewalks should be at least 5 feet (1.52 meters) wide in residential areas and 9 to 12 feet (2.74 to 3.66 meters) in mixed-use and commercial areas. Parkway strips or a "street furniture zone" of 5 to 10 feet (1.52 to 3.05 meters) can buffer pedestrians from traffic and allow tree planting, mailboxes, and streetlights. Crosswalks should be provided mid-block if the blocks are longer than 300 feet (91.44 meters).

*Source:* Adapted from Local Government Commission and Steve Tracy, *Smart Growth Zoning Codes,* 2003.

# Planning and Visioning

As mentioned at many points throughout this text, it is crucial that stakeholders and community members share a common vision. The following planning and visioning tools provide different ways of creating or communicating a common vision to the community.

## Community Visioning Workshops and Charrettes

Community visioning workshops and charrettes are techniques that help stakeholders envision the outcome of future development. They are often invaluable to gaining community buy-in to concepts such as compact development. Presenting illustrations of possible projects is often a highly successful approach to overcoming initial caution. In particular, visioning workshops (often more broadly based for a neighborhood, city, or region) and charrettes (more likely to be project-specific) can be very effective.

Community visioning workshops and charrettes can help communities evaluate how they want to grow, what they want the growth to look like, and how to make policy choices to support the vision. They can range in length from a few hours to multiday events. Visioning workshops can be used in a variety of planning efforts, such as community planning and transportation studies. The many benefits to visioning workshops include the following:

■ Actively engaging citizens, offering them opportunities to contribute their own thoughts and ideas as well as to learn from the planning professionals and designers;
■ Gathering an array of stakeholders in a "team-building" environment, and helping them overcome possibly divisive issues; and

■ Early timing, holding workshops early in the planning process, to gain community buy-in and sort out concerns before they grow to be major issues.

The interactive approach to planning that visioning workshops and charrettes can foster is an excellent opportunity for participants to discuss a variety of options for community growth and development and contribute to comprehensive planning for a particular site, neighborhood, or locality. As such, it can be a worthwhile setting for local planners or advocates to introduce and explore the prospect of higher-density housing. The visual nature of these workshops also allows participants to examine more closely what higher-density housing actually looks like, embrace new possibilities, and overcome potential objections. Off-site field trips to view actual examples of nearby development can often help those who have difficulty envisioning design concepts from a one-dimensional presentation.

## Keys to Success

Successful charrettes and visioning workshops are built on strong leadership and excellent communication skills; however, follow-through and implementation are critical if the results of the process are to be actualized. Communities organizing such events should keep in mind the following:

■ Assemble a strong team to lead the effort. A strategic steering committee with diverse local membership, as well as possibly an outside consultant with needed skills and experience, is important to manage the project successfully.
■ Implement a comprehensive outreach and publicity plan to attract broad-based community participation. A vision that reflects the involvement of a variety of representatives from the

community will earn more widespread buy-in and ultimately be more useful.

- Plan for the future. The effort to coalesce a successful visioning effort should be sufficiently ambitious. A community vision should consider the next ten to 20 years in addition to the next three to five.

- Put pictures in the vision. Not just the process but the final product should have a visual component—such as images, drawings, or photographs—to easily communicate the vision.

- Ensure follow-through and implementation. After a successful visioning and charrette have been completed, staff and local leadership frequently are the ones to take the necessary steps to realize the vision.

- Ensure that staff members have the skills to implement the vision. Even if a consultant managed the actual visioning workshop, is it important to have a planner or other professional with training in urban design who has the skills and abilities to translate the vision into actual code changes that will encourage compact development, keep plans on track, and review development proposals to ensure their compatibility with the community vision.

## Examples and Resources

### Suffield, Connecticut, Community Visioning Workshop
http://www.suffieldtownhall.com/content/85/169/default.aspx

The town of Suffield, population 12,000, about 25 miles (40.23 km) north of Hartford, was a pilot demonstration community visioning project for the Hartford-based Capitol Region Council of Government's Livable Communities project. Participants included a cross section of elected officials, civic leaders, citizens' groups, the plan-ning and zoning commission, and attendees at a public town festival. The product of the effort was a town plan that directed development to the town center and other urbanized areas while preserving its rural landscapes elsewhere. In turn, the town has modified its zoning, increased agricultural land preservation efforts, and undertaken streetscape improvements. Because of the visioning process, the town's zoning changes have included a mixed-use overlay zone for the village center, an architectural design review process, agricultural zoning, and shared parking in the town center.

### Florida Department of Community Affairs Visioning and Facilitation Services
http://www.dca.state.fl.us/fdcp/dcp/visioning/index.cfm

Florida growth management laws encourage local governments to establish a community vision to guide land use planning. To support local visioning efforts, the Department of Community Affairs provides technical assistance, publications, and guidance to help local governments design, organize, and facilitate visioning workshops.

### Treasure Coast, Florida, Urban Design Studio
http://www.tcrpc.org/departments/studio.html

Florida's Treasure Coast Regional Planning Council (TCRPC) Urban Design Studio provides assistance to its local communities in considering land use and transportation planning issues. TCRPC has also worked with other regional planning councils to convene charrettes in Dade, Broward, Flagler, and Polk counties. Each charrette lasts seven to ten days, during which time a team of designers works with stakeholders to produce a community master plan.

### Teton County, Wyoming, Community Charrette
http://www.tetonwyo.org/housing/docs/
section%20i-introduction.htm

In 2001, rural Teton County in Wyoming convened a weeklong community charrette to address transportation and land use issues in the town of Wilson. Nearly 130 participants considered roadway design alternatives, pedestrian and bicycle access, future land use designations, and how to maintain housing affordability during the course of a series of public presentations and workshops. The community developed a vision for a mixed-use village, with high-density uses at the center of town.

### Urban Land Institute Reality Check Guide
http://www.uli.org/realitycheckguide

Reality Check is a regional visioning program developed by the Urban Land Institute to assist ULI District Councils and their partners to plan, build upon, and implement regional exercises and visions. Reality Check is a one-day participatory visioning exercise created by ULI Los Angeles and inspired by Envision Utah to engage regional leaders in a regional dialogue on growth issues.

## Density Visualization

Converting technical project plans and planning terminology into illustrations can be a powerful way to communicate with stakeholders, public officials, and developers. In addition to software tools that can create lifelike renderings of future development, a variety of online databases and other resources can help people visualize density. The following are some examples of resources and tools that can help people understand what density can look like.

## Examples and Resources

### CommunityViz Software
http://www.communityviz.com/

CommunityViz is advanced yet easy-to-use GIS (Geographic Information Systems) software designed to help people visualize, analyze, and communicate about important land use decisions. Operating as an extension to ESRI's ArcGIS platform, CommunityViz allows users to create three-dimensional visual models of future scenarios, interactive analysis of development choices, and other decision-making tools.

### Neighborhood Explorations: This View of Density
http://www.sflcv.org/density/

The San Francisco League of Conservation Voters has created a density calculator with images that illustrate various land use patterns, their effects on travel behavior, and environmental impacts.

### Pedestrian and Bicycle Information Center Image Library
http://www.pedbikeimages.org

This Web site features a comprehensive image library of bicycle- and pedestrian-friendly environments with a category for compact development.

### Visualizing Density
http://www.lincolninst.edu/subcenters/VD/

Published by the Lincoln Institute of Land Policy in 2007, *Visualizing Density* includes an essay on the density challenge facing the United States, an illustrated manual on planning and designing for "good" density, and a catalog of more than 250 diverse neighborhoods across the country, noting density in housing units per acre for each site. Four photographs of each location are included—close-up, context, neighborhood, and plan views—to provide an impartial and comparative view of the many ways to design neighborhoods. A corresponding interactive Web site provides a variety of resources to help understand high-quality dense development.

## Transect-Based Planning

Transect-based planning is an effort to reinvent conventional planning and zoning that regulates land by single uses, with some overlap with form-based codes. Transect-based planning divides a community into six zones, ranging from urban to rural. Each of these zones accommodates a mix of land uses, with higher densities for residential and commercial uses at the core that gradually decrease toward the edge. The zones are

- Urban Core—a central business district;
- Urban Center—a neighborhood or town center;
- General Urban—primarily residential, but with higher densities, a variety of housing types, and some mixed uses;
- Edge/Suburban—a transition zone between countryside and town, mostly with single-family residential uses;
- Rural Reserve—areas that may warrant protection in the future; and
- Rural Preserve—protected areas.

Each zone contains specifications for natural features, buildings, and characteristics of the physical environment, such as density, streets, buildings, lighting, and parks.

### How Can Transect-Based Planning Support Compact Development?

Transect-based planning seeks to transform traditional approaches to land use in part by directing higher-intensity uses to the core, center, and general zones. These zones are designed both to accommodate higher-density residential housing types and to absorb mixed uses and a range of transportation options. Adopting a transect-based planning approach can help communities clearly designate where higher densities are welcome, as well as channel appropriate infrastructure and commercial and retail uses to accompany multifamily housing.

Transect-based planning is likely to require a major reconstitution of local planning and zoning. As with any major change in a community's land use regulations, involving the public, obtaining appropriate professional expertise, ensuring support from local leaders, and arranging for appropriate implementation are all critical. The SmartCode developed by the new urbanist firms Duany Plater Zyberk and PlaceMakers (see "Form-Based Codes") has been developed as a model code for transect-based planning.

### Example

**Miami 21 Plan**
http://www.miami21.org

As part of its Miami 21 plan, the city of Miami has undertaken transect-based planning to provide an urban design orientation in its planning practices. The city has identified a series of neighborhoods, corridors, urban centers, and districts, each with its own arrangement of transect zones. With the transect approach, the code focuses on pedestrians, public spaces, access to open spaces, transitions in density and height between buildings, and mass transit.

# Bibliography and Resources

Arrington, G. B. "Light Rail and the American City: The State-of-the-Practice for TOD." *Transportation Research Circular EC508.* Washington, D.C.: Transportation Research Board, 2003.

Bohl, Charles. *Place Making and Town Center Development.* Washington, D.C.: Urban Land Institute, 2003.

Bruce, Laura, and Kaid Benfield. *Existing Endorsement and Rating Systems for "Smart" Development with Reference to Best Development Practices.* Washington, D.C.: Natural Resources Defense Council, 2004. http://docs. nrdc.org/cities/cit_06080902A.pdf.

*Compact Development CD: A Toolkit to Build Support for Higher Density Housing.* Sacramento, Calif.: Local Government Commission, 2002. http://www2.lgc. org/bookstore/detail.cfm?categoryId=1&typeId=0&item Id=33.

Ewing, Reid H. *Growing Cooler: The Evidence on Urban Development and Climate Change.* Washington, D.C.: Urban Land Institute, 2008.

Fader, Steven. *Density by Design: New Directions in Residential Development.* Washington, D.C.: Urban Land Institute, 2000.

Federal Highway Administration. "Tool Kit for Integrating Land Use and Transportation Decision-Making." http:// www.fhwa.dot.gov/planning/landuse/index.htm.

Garvin, Elizabeth A. "Unraveling the Mysteries of Code Writing." *Planning* (Summer 2003). http://www. planning.org/thecommissioner/summer03.htm.

Georgia Quality Growth Project. *Toolkit of Best Practices.* http://www.dca.state.ga.us/toolkit/.

*Getting to Smart Growth: 100 Policies for Implementation.* Smart Growth Network and International City/ County Management Association, 2002. http://www. smartgrowth.org/pdf/gettosg.pdf.

*Getting to Smart Growth II: 100 More Policies for Implementation.* Smart Growth Network and International City/County Management Association, 2003. http:// www.epa.gov/smartgrowth/getting_to_sg2.htm.

Green, Gary, Anna Haines, and Stephen Halebsky. *Building Our Future: A Guide to Community Visioning.* Madison: University of Wisconsin Extension, 2000.

Gupta, Prema Katari, and Kathryn Terzano. *Creating Great Town Centers and Urban Villages.* Washington, D.C.: Urban Land Institute, 2008.

Haughey, Richard M. *Higher-Density Development: Myth and Fact.* Washington, D.C.: Urban Land Institute, 2005.

Holtzclaw, John. "Community Characteristics Promoting Transit and Walking." [updated March 2007] (from "Using Residential Patterns and Transit to Decrease Auto Dependence and Costs"; Natural Resources Defense Council, June 1994). http://www.sierraclub.org/sprawl/ articles/characteristics.asp.

*Integration of Land Use and Transportation Planning: Lessons Learned from the Second Domestic Scan Tour*. Prepared by the SCAN team for the Office of Planning, Federal Highway Administration, U.S. Department of Transportation, Washington, D.C., May 2004. http://www.planning.dot.gov/Documents/DomesticScan/domscan2.htm.

*Land Use and Transportation Coordination: Lessons Learned from Domestic Scan Tour*. Prepared by the SCAN team for the Office of Planning, Federal Highway Administration, U.S. Department of Transportation, Washington, D.C., March 2003. http://www.planning.dot.gov/Documents/DomesticScan/domscan603.htm.

Schwanke, Dean, et al. *Mixed-Use Development Handbook*. Washington, D.C.: Urban Land Institute, 2003.

Local Government Commission in cooperation with U.S. EPA. *Creating Great Neighborhoods: Density in Your Community*. Washington, D.C.: National Association of Realtors, 2003.

Metropolitan Council (Minneapolis–St. Paul). "Guide for Transit-Oriented Development." August 2006. http://www.metrocouncil.org/planning/TOD/tod.htm.

Mix, Troy D. "Exploring the Benefits of Compact Development." Delaware Office of State Planning Coordination, Wilmington, August 2003.

National Governors Association. *Growth and Quality of Life Tool Kit*. Washington, D.C.: NGA Center for Best Practices, 2001. www.nga.org.

Patton, Zach. "Back on Track: Sprawling Sun Belt Cities Discover a New Way to Grow." *Governing* 20, no. 9 (2007).

Pedestrian Bicycle Information Center Image Library. *Compact Developments Pictures*. http://www.pedbikeimages.org/category_front.cfm?categoryId=69.

Purcell, Nichole. "Statewide Planning: A National Overview." *Creating Communities of Place: New Jersey Office of State Planning Memo* 3, no. 2 (March 1997).

Research Department, American Planning Association. *Model Smart Land Development Regulations*. Chicago: American Planning Associaion, 2006. http://www.planning.org/smartgrowthcodes/phase1.htm#1.

Sacramento Area Council of Governments. "The Seven Principles of Smart Growth: Examples from the Sacramento Region of Better Ways to Grow." Sacramento, California, April 2004. http://www.sacog.org/regionalfunding/betterways.pdf.

Schmitz, Adrienne. *Multifamily Housing Development Handbook*. ULI development handbook series. Washington, D.C.: Urban Land Institute, 2000.

Sitkowski, Robert, and Brian Ohm. "Form-Based Land Development Regulations." *Urban Lawyer* 28, no.1 (Winter 2006).

Smart Growth Network. "Smart Growth Online." http://www.smartgrowth.org.

Tombari, Edward A. "Smart Growth, Smart Choices Series: Mixed-Use Development." National Association of Home Builders, Washington, D.C., January 2005.

Tompkins County Planning Department (New York). "Vital Communities Toolbox." http://www.co.tompkins.ny.us/planning/vct/index.html.

Tracy, Steve. *Smart Growth Zoning Codes: A Resource Guide*. Sacramento, Calif.: Local Government Commission, 2003.

Wells, Barbara. *Smart Growth at the Frontier: Strategies and Resources for Rural Communities*. Washington, D.C.: Northeast-Midwest Institute, 2002.

West Coast Environmental Law Research Foundation. *Smart Bylaws Guide*. Vancouver, BC. http://www.wcel.org/issues/urban/sbg/.